ROME TO ROSEBURG

ROME TO ROSEBURG:

Oma In Oregon, The Transformation of One Woman's Life

HILDE BAUGHMAN

ISBN Paperback: 978-1-7368728-9-5
ISBN Ebook: 978-1-7368728-8-8

Hilde Baughman
125 Reiten Drive, Ashland Oregon 97520
541- 482-5934
Email: hildegaustadt@gmail.com

Cover Art: Ty McGee
Interior Design: Sue Balcer

Note

More than half my life ago I began collecting brief quotes from books (ranging from Leo Tolstoy to Hunter Thompson), and from various other sources (poems, essays, movies, songs). I've included some of them here - excerpts offered not as assertions of truth, but meant to provoke thought and query.

My husband-author Mike served as a helpful editor throughout the writing of this book, which I dedicate to him with all my love.

H. B.

CONTENTS

WRAPPED IN MY BLANKET
WITH LOTTE

A thought comes to mind often these days: In 1964 I did some modeling in San Francisco. Two years later my husband Mike and I moved to Oregon, and as time passed I traded in my nylons, stylish dresses and silk blouses for jeans, sweatshirts and chest waders, and my stiletto high heels for hiking and cross-country ski boots, water sandals and running shoes. Now I'm an Oma (grandma) from Germany, still living in Oregon. No heads turn when I walk into a room – unless somebody wants a good look at an old woman - and I like it that way. I'm who and where I want to be and I still love my life, and this is how things happened:

In the spring of 1945 I was six years old, and, in my memory, I can still hear nighttime sirens howling. Airplanes were on their way, and we had to hurry to the bomb shelter. I had no idea why there was a war or where Russia was, but I knew that because of the war my father was a prisoner there. My brother Herbert was a year younger than me, and my mother, holding our hands, led us up a hill along a narrow cobblestone road. Ahead of us and behind us, other family groups hurried along, many people clutching blankets. It was cold any time of year in a

Felsenkeller (stone cellar), which was what we called the bomb shelter. Wrapped in my blanket was Lotte, my favorite doll. It took no more than ten minutes to reach the shelter from our house. A steep flight of stairs led from the doorway down to a long, narrow room with wooden benches along both walls. At the far end of the room was the door to a toilet. The only light came from a few dim bulbs spaced along the ceiling.

There were mostly women and children there, along with a few old men. We sat pressed against each other on the benches. Latecomers had to stand. Some women cried, many held rosaries in their hands, and people joined together to say their *Vater unsers* (Our Fathers). Sometimes we heard airplanes flying overhead, and then, a little later, the sounds of explosions. I sat close beside my mother, frightened, wrapped in my blanket with Lotte.

Women see war for what it is – a matter of broken bodies and crying mothers.

Alexander McCall Smith

AN ORANGE AND A
CHOCOLATE BAR

In 1938 I was born in the thousand-year-old Catholic town of Bamberg, state of Bavaria, region of Franconia. Built on seven hills, Bamberg is known as the Franconian Rome. The bomb shelter I remember wasn't far from the house my father had finished building shortly before he was taken into the army to serve as a medic. Decades later in Oregon, watching the history channel, I learned that, toward the end of the war in Europe, Bamberg had been selected as a nighttime bombing target. It wasn't an industrial town and had little or nothing to do with supplying the German army, but at that late stage of the fighting America and its allies wanted to inflict punishment, and Bamberg, compact and densely populated, made an ideal target. We were saved by a heavy cloud cover that blanketed the town, forcing the bombers to strike somewhere else. I'm sure I was in the shelter with Lotte that night.

The American soldiers who occupied Bamberg after the war treated us kindly. One of the two soldiers who temporarily lived on the second floor of our house was the first black man I'd ever seen, and he gave me two treats I'd never enjoyed before – an orange and a chocolate bar. Not long after that my father returned home by train and was overjoyed when, just before reaching the *Bahnhof* (train station), he could see that the house he had built near the top of a hill was still standing. He soon took his old job back at the hospital near the bottom of the same hill, alongside the Regnitz River.

By the time my father came home I was a student at the Catholic *Volkschule* (elementary school). After that came *Mittleschule,* and finally *Handelsschule* (business school) where nuns, many of whom inflicted strict discipline, taught girls shorthand, typing, business terminology, and also English, in preparation for the secretarial work we were likely to find. I was called a bright student, but in those days very few females from working class families attended universities. I was too naïve to feel deprived because of that, and I enjoyed my postwar life.

My brother Herbert and I rode hundreds of kilometers on our bikes, along the paved path on the river bank and the dirt roads that connected Bamberg to nearby villages, where we had grandparents, aunts, uncles and cousins to visit. I swam in the river and joined a girls' gymnastic group. When my sister Elisabeth was born, two years after my father returned home, I was glad to be old enough to help my mother around the house and in the large vegetable garden that had helped get us through the war.

Many American soldiers were stationed in the former German army barracks on the outskirts of Bamberg. Whenever my friends and I walked or rode our bikes to town, often to see a movie, we saw them, sometimes noisy and drunk, but never threatening. What surprised us most, and puzzled us, was the way they were dressed in wintertime. On the coldest days they wore what we saw as light summer clothing and, hands jammed into their pockets, sometimes noticeably shivering, they appeared to be on the verge of freezing. We wondered if they'd all come to Germany from Florida or California, the warm and sunny places we sometimes saw in American movies. Many Germans called the American soldiers "*Amis*" (pronounced Ahmees), and I learned that some of them called us "Krauts."

As a teenager my life inevitably began to change. I enrolled at a *Tanzkurs* (dance school) and learned to waltz to Johann Strauss, and also to tango and foxtrot. I became a good dancer, and I knew I was attractive. The boys at the school affirmed this when they lined up to ask me to dance.

I began meeting people outside my family and circle of friends. An elderly couple, Herr and Frau Wolff, originally from Poland, lived in the neighborhood. He had been the rector of a school and she had been an English teacher. My mother and I were on a weekend walk to a neighboring village, and when we crossed paths they introduced themselves. After that I began to visit them at home, where they tutored me in English and gave me books to read. The father of a school friend of mine, Christiana, was a member of the well known Bamberg Symphony Orchestra. He invited me to attend concerts, and I loved the music and learned about it. These were the adults who introduced me to areas of life I most likely wouldn't have experienced otherwise.

I remember my excitement when, at age sixteen, I prepared to attend my first formal dance at the ballroom in town. Later in life, when I read *War and Peace,* Natasha's exhilaration reminded me of what I'd felt. I searched hard and chose what struck me as a beautiful gown, and the right petticoats to go with it. I spent an hour or more carefully arranging my hair, and almost as long applying makeup. Would anybody ask me to dance? Probably – almost certainly - but who? Like Natasha, I had nothing to fear, and the night seemed wonderful.

There was a general feeling of optimism among Germans of all ages through the 1950s. The war was in the past, and virtually all conditions of daily life were steadily improving. Cities and towns were being rebuilt, family incomes were growing, jobs were available, people enjoyed summer vacations. In 1957, when I was eighteen, I took a job in Bamberg as a secretary for a textile union. My parents gave me what amounted to a private apartment on the first floor of the family house. I liked my job, and had an income, and something close to independence.

ONE OF THE AMIS
APPEALED TO ME

Virtually all varieties of German employees were (and still are) guaranteed six weeks of paid vacation per year, usually divided into three weeks in summer and three in winter. In groups of young people travelling by bus, I visited Austria, Holland, northern Italy, Paris, and Belgium during its World Fair.

Traveling to different countries taught me things. I was prepared for the fact that there would be French people not well disposed toward Germans, and I understood. On a summer evening in Paris our group visited a wine bar where there was dancing. When some handsome young Algerian men tried to enter the place, to my surprise and disappointment the maitre d' turned them away. I didn't fall in love with the handsome Italian I met in Venice, but I liked him very much, and we spent both days and evenings together and did what healthy young humans who like each other do. I felt complimented when he came to the train station to see me off on my return to Germany. A few minutes after we kissed goodbye I looked out the train window for him, and saw him talking enthusiastically to a pretty blond, probably another German, who had just stepped off a train from the north.

In Bamberg I had an active social life, and a few relationships with boys that qualified as romances, but nothing truly serious. There was a university in Bamberg, established in 1647, and another university half an hour away in Erlangen. I dated a student from Erlangen, and when that ended I wanted to meet more students, especially boys, so in 1959 I joined an International Students Club in a large three-story house in Hain Park near the river. It was the former residence of Colonel Klaus Von Stauffenberg, who in July, 1944, had been executed by a firing squad after his failed attempt to assassinate Hitler. His widow Nina donated the building and established the club to promote friendship among different nationalities. The ground floor held a restaurant and bar along with space to dance. On the upper floors were a library, a chess room, and a comfortable lounge with ping pong tables.

Students who visited the club came from all over Europe and beyond, making it a lively and interesting place. There were often a few Americans, most of them former students, and nearly every one of them I met explained that they hated the popular GI bars in town, and that the International Club was a welcome alternative.

On a cold night in February, 1960, a girlfriend and I attended evening mass at Saint Martin's Cathedral in downtown Bamberg. I don't remember what his subject was, but the priest talked longer than usual. We hurried toward the bus stop after the service, but were still a block away when we saw our bus pulling away.

On a Sunday night the next bus wouldn't come by for an hour, and, to stay warm, we decided to visit the

International Club, a short walk away. When Elfie and I walked in I saw a few couples dancing to recorded music. Half the tables were occupied, including four Americans with glasses of wine in front of them near the back of the room. At first glance, one of the *Amis* appealed to me. When our eyes met, I looked away first.

Elfie and I sat at an empty table and ordered glasses of *Frankenwein*. As soon as the waiter turned to leave, Mike stepped up to the table and asked me to dance. We danced, and talked in English, and fell in love. How can such things happen? I have no clear or rational idea, and I don't think anybody does. Sixteen months later I became his wife.

Except for the two of us, our relationship made little or no sense to anybody. I'd lived in the same town, and the same house, all my life, and Mike had grown up in Hawaii, exactly half a world away. After playing college football in Boston he and a friend had hitchhiked back and forth across America, to see and get to know the country. My parents weren't pleased to learn that I was serious about an *Ami* with no clear prospects for his future. I liked my job and he was looking forward to working his way through graduate school after his discharge, but with no clear idea what might happen after that. Even strangers made it known that they didn't appreciate our liaison. At a *Gasthaus* in Munich an angry young man who had probably had too much beer called me a traitor for dating an *Ami*.

My father was a soccer referee on weekends, and Mike played on the Warner Barracks basketball team. I'd never seen the sport before and knew nothing about it, but watched his games and figured it out. Basketball could be seen as soccer played with hands instead of feet in a small indoor area with a big ball, small goals and high scores.

We went out to dinner and drank wine and beer and danced in well chosen places in town. After I introduced Mike to the Schlenkerla, a *Gasthaus* famous for its smoked beer, we went there often. Customers commonly shared tables with strangers, creating an atmosphere of relaxed geniality that Germans call *Gemutlichkeit*. We took long weekend walks from Bamberg to neighboring villages. We sat on benches in Hain Park and read poetry. Sometimes we argued. (After sixty-one years of marriage we still argue, but everybody does that.)

We spent a long winter weekend in Reit im Winkl, a German ski village near the Austrian border. We learned to downhill ski together, and on our last day there overestimated our skills. After carrying our skis and poles up a steep mountain to the summit, we rightly decided to carry the skis and poles back down. But we loved Reit im Winkl, streets packed with cold, clean snow and *Gasthauses* and *Weinstuben* warm and inviting. We loved each other under feather quilts in a cold room with a view of the mountains.

In mid-summer Mike took a two-week leave and I took two weeks of my vacation. I lied to my family and told them I was visiting Italy with my close friend, Ingrid. Mike and I rode a train to Naples and took a boat from there to the magical island of Capri. A funicular car ran from the Capri docks to the top of a hill, where we stayed in a comfortable *pension* room with a view of the Mediterranean. There were no cars on the heights of the island, and the narrow pedestrian lanes wound through homes, shops and restaurants, with flowers everywhere. After breakfast we walked down a steep trail to the sea and spent most of every day on one beach or another. Mike had brought the equipment and taught me to snorkel. The underwater life I saw, my first exposure to true wildness, created fear of the unknown at first, and then excitement and exhilaration.

On our way back to Germany we stopped in Rome for two days where we made wishes and threw German, Italian and American coins into the Trevi Fountain, and enjoyed the Via Veneto nightlife. On the train back to Germany Mike told me he felt more depressed than he ever had in his life, obliged to return to the barracks after the two weeks we'd spent together. Back at home my mother told me that while I was gone, in downtown Bamberg, she'd run into Ingrid, the friend I was supposed to have been with in Italy. I could explain it only by telling her the truth I knew would hurt her. I was in love with my *Ami,* and we planned to be married.

When Mike told his battalion personnel officer that he wanted to fill out the papers that would permit him to marry a German citizen, the response he got surprised him. The officer, a Japanese American, a naturalized citizen, suggested he might be making a big mistake and should think hard about it before deciding not to marry an American girl. A Catholic priest told me I could be making a big mistake by marrying a man with a different religion, language and nationality. We paid no attention and were married in May, 1961, in the Bamberger *Dom,* a cathedral founded in 1002. My parents had accepted my decision, and Mike's mother came from California for the wedding.

———————————

At one of my prewar lectures – and they were damned bold for the times – on the basis of that quotation from Faust I developed the melancholy notion that there is no such thing as happiness, that it is either unattainable or illusory. And then a student handed up a note written on a piece of graph paper from a tiny notebook: "But I am in love - and I am happy!" How do you answer that?

ALEXANDER SOLZHENITSYN, *THE FIRST CIRCLE*

———————————

WONDER BREAD OR
BUDWEISER

In August, 1961, construction of the Berlin Wall began, and in September Mike boarded a troop ship that carried him from Hamburg to New York. Birth control was less reliable then than it is now, and I was pregnant.

We timed it so that I'd arrive in New York two days after Mike did. My parents drove me to the Frankfurt Airport. On the way there my mother told me that when she was young a boy she knew emigrated to America and didn't return to Bamberg for fifty years. I promised her I'd be back to visit soon. We all cried saying goodbye, and I was very nervous, even frightened. I'd never left home for any length of time or been in an airplane before. Jet travel wasn't generally available then, and the plane made refueling stops in Ireland and Newfoundland.

Thanks to the military, Mike had a comfortable room in a midtown Manhattan hotel and two tickets to the Broadway musical "My Fair Lady" the night I arrived. I was exhausted from the long flight along with the time difference, and fell asleep before intermission. What I remember about New York are crowded streets, tall buildings, and cheesecake at a restaurant named Lindy's. The next morning we boarded a flight to Oakland that, with three stops, lasted more than eighteen hours. One of the stops was in Wichita, Kansas, and the view from the airplane window as we landed revealed the bleakest landscape I'd ever seen. Mike's parents picked us up at the Oakland Airport after dark, and, in contrast to Wichita, on the drive across the Bay Bridge to San Francisco the bright city lights were beautiful.

Mike had a week of leave time before his date to report for his last few months of army duty at Fort Ord, near Monterey, more than a hundred miles south of San Francisco. We spent the week in his parent's large, comfortable San Francisco apartment. Once I was rested, I liked the city – the hills, the cable cars, the bridges, the views of the bay, Golden Gate Park, the restaurants his parents took us to. It was a new, exciting world. When we walked along Grant Avenue to Kan's Restaurant in ChinaTown I saw my first Asians, hundreds of them. There were people of all shades and ethnicities nearly everywhere we went, wearing everything from tuxedos to turbans. The cars were twice the size of what I was used to, and I didn't see any identifiable Germans or hear or see the German language anywhere. I was equal parts homesick and thrilled.

Mike's parents gifted us with a used black Pontiac sedan. Serious homesickness came after the drive to Monterey, and for a week or two I cried every day. The best affordable place we could find to live was a few blocks from the ocean, a tiny second-floor apartment with a kitchen and bathroom, the living room so small that when the Murphy bed was lowered out of the wall the front door couldn't be opened. Sometimes Mike had to start for

Fort Ord at 5:40 a.m. for an early basketball practice. He couldn't leave through a window, and, being pregnant, I couldn't risk lowering the heavy bed myself, so I had to get up and stay up at that hour whether I wanted to or not.

We had a few pots, pans, plates, dishes and silverware, a radio, a cheap phonograph, three long-play records, some books (a few of them in German), some sheets, blankets and towels. Our army pay budget allowed us enough spare money to go out for one pizza and one movie a month. We bought a *San Francisco Chronicle* every Sunday.

When he wasn't playing basketball or volleyball for the Fort Ord teams Mike did clerical work. One evening he came home and told me he'd been typing orders that would soon send hundreds of soldiers to Vietnam. Neither of us had any precise idea of where the country was or why Americans were going there.

I was assigned a doctor at Fort Ord to care for me during my pregnancy, and I missed my family, especially my mother. I wanted her to be with me. We wrote long letters back and forth, our only way to communicate, because my parents didn't yet have a phone.

I did my best to adjust to life in Monterey and made connections with other international army wives in our apartment house. Kim, from Korea, proudly served us her very spicy specialty, kimchi. Anita, from Germany, was married to a soldier from Guam who wanted rice with every meal, even breakfast. They brought it home in twenty-pound bags from the Fort Ord commissary. Gabby, an American from Ohio, had a husband who gave her a hard time for driving to church on Sunday after he'd seen me walking there, knowing I was pregnant.

Our apartment was two blocks from the Pacific Ocean. On the long beach walks we took I enjoyed the ocean view, the shells we sometimes found, and the sounds of seals barking like dogs near the Monterey pier. On an especially nice day with the tide low we extended our walk to a mile or more south of town. The mood was ruined when a mean man on a horse suddenly appeared, wearing the kind of cowboy hat I'd seen only in movies, and wearing a holstered gun along with it. Walking at the water's edge with the tide low, we'd missed the "no trespassing" sign nailed to a fence post. We walked back, the mounted cowboy a few yards behind us all the way.

Small problems sometimes took my mind off my homesickness. I hated the Wonder Bread sold at the commissary. It was mushy and had no real crust, or flavor, and to me the wonder was that anybody would eat it. Mike hated American beer because, compared to the smoked beer at the *Schlenkerla* in Bamberg, it had no more taste than carbonated water. I remember an enjoyable extended argument we had about which product was worse, Wonder Bread or Budweiser.

The Pacific Ocean was too cold for comfortable swimming, so on warm weekend days we often wore bathing suits to Monterey motels to swim and sit in poolside chairs or lounges, as if we were paying guests. As our confidence grew we went to bigger pools at nicer motels, where we could dry off in the warm sun on a shuffleboard court between swims. When we finally tried one of the most expensive places in town, we took chairs near an exit to the street, hoping we wouldn't be noticed. But not long after we sat down an important looking man wearing a suit and tie approached us with a serious look on his face.

"I think he'll kick us out," Mike said to me under his breath. "Don't worry though. We haven't broken any serious laws."

The man stopped, and looked me over and smiled. "Are you comfortable here?" he asked.

I nodded my head and tried to smile back.

He looked at Mike. "If you'd like, I'll find you places closer to the pool."

"We're fine here," Mike answered. "Thanks for the offer though."

"I like to see young guests at our establishment. Enjoy yourselves. Just let us know if there's anything we can do for you."

We enjoyed ourselves late into the afternoon and never went back.

And we ended up liking Monterey. During our months there we made future plans. Once he was discharged in May, Mike would find a decent paying job in San Francisco, and we'd stay with his parents until we found a suitable apartment for ourselves and our child. In September Mike would start night classes at San Francisco State College and work toward a Master's Degree in English Language Arts with an emphasis in creative writing. Instate tuition was $96 per year and, according to ads in the *Chronicle,* we'd have no problem finding a comfortable apartment for something between $100 and $150 per month.

I saw my doctor once every month. He'd advised me not to gain more than two pounds per month, and I didn't. I was careful with my diet, and my health was good. The only problem was that Mike would be discharged on May 14th, and my due-date was mid-May. If the baby arrived after the 14th, the army wouldn't be responsible for the delivery. We ended up making provisional plans at a San Francisco hospital.

On the afternoon of May 11th, a Thursday, we took a long, slow walk up and down the beach, careful not to trespass. After that we visited a motel and played shuffleboard for more than an hour. Either our idea worked or we were lucky. I went into labor that evening, and our son Pete was born that night. On May 15th we headed north to San Francisco with Pete wrapped in a blanket in a laundry basket on the back seat of our old Pontiac.

―――――――――

There is a secret in our culture, and it's not that childbirth is painful. It's that women are strong.

Laura Staove Harm

―――――――――

With his father's help Mike got a decent-paying union job (about $400 per month) as a "miscellaneous helper" at a wholesale meat market. We were lucky enough to find a two-bedroom apartment on Funston Avenue in the

Sunset District, three blocks from Golden Gate Park and a short drive from San Francisco State. When we went to look at the place the landlady told us she'd already agreed to rent it to someone else, but when she heard my accent and asked where I was from, she decided to rent it to us, for $135 per month. "I can't go wrong with a German housekeeper," she said.

Our time in San Francisco went well despite our circumstances. My in-laws were happy to babysit their grandson whenever we asked them to. Out walking with Pete in a stroller, often in Golden Gate Park, I met young mothers from our neighborhood. We soon formed a babysitting cooperative and began to socialize together as families. Through his first year of graduate school Mike worked for eight hours a day in a huge refrigerated room, carrying sides of beef, pitch-forking hunks of beef into a huge meat grinder, and packaging steaks, chops, ground beef and roasts for delivery to restaurants. Four nights a week, Mondays through Thursdays, he attended three-hour classes at San Francisco State.

That summer I took my first flight home with my one-year-old son Pete. My father was building an addition to the house, and on warm days I sometimes sat outside and talked to him as he worked. When Pete was with me he played with a nearby pile of pebbles, and the first word he ever spoke was *Stein* – German for stone. Because I'd decided to stay for three months, my parents wondered if I really wanted to go back. I assured them that I did. I'd always miss Bamberg but at the same time realized it wasn't as perfect as I'd tried to make it in my mind. I was glad when the time came for Pete and me to return to my husband and our San Francisco life.

You will never be completely at home again, because part of your heart always will be elsewhere. This is the price you pay for the richness of loving and knowing people in more than one place.

MIRIAM ADENEY

NO TRACE OF CIVILIZATION
ANYWHERE

Our plan for Mike's second year of school was for me to find work, hopefully with pay close to what he made at Davidson Meat Company. While I worked Mike would care for Pete, do school work, and write the short novel that would be his dissertation.

I'd had a recommendation written by my boss in Germany translated into English, but when I told my father in law I'd applied at Fireman's Fund Insurance Company he was skeptical. "Don't expect to get hired the first place you apply," he said. "There's plenty of competition out there." For my interview I dressed in my best German work uniform – blouse, pencil skirt, nylons and high-heeled shoes. I got the job, the pay was enough, and I did my work well. In an entire year I made only one serious mistake with language that I can remember. When I typed up a letter dictated to me by my boss, I substituted "feed bag" for "feedback." He was kind enough to laugh at the blunder. Not long after that someone somewhere noticed me. I never learned who it was or where it happened, but our income improved when I ended up hired to do some modeling at evening fashion shows.

In the 1960s most of what we wanted to do in San Francisco was affordable – plays like "Who's Afraid of Virginia Woolf," performances by popular singers like Nat King Cole and jazz musicians like Cannonball Adderley. We could afford occasional tickets to Major League Baseball, NBA Basketball, and NFL football games. Better yet, there was free cultural entertainment. Hippies made their appearance while we were in town. The Sunset District borders the Haight-Ashbury, and not long after the hippies arrived there were bus tours along Haight Street offering tourists a look at the nonconforming newcomers. But the hippies soon began approaching the buses with large mirrors, so that what the tourists saw was themselves.

San Francisco was as beautiful as most European cities I'd visited, and I found myself sorry to leave. Mike had applied for teaching jobs and, probably thanks to strong recommendations and the fact that his short novel won a local literary prize, he was offered jobs in locations ranging all the way from Florida to Hawaii. We ended up choosing Southern Oregon College in Ashland. When he visited for an interview he liked the school, the town and the countryside.

On an early Sunday morning in August we crossed the Bay Bridge and started north in our Pontiac, towing a small U-haul trailer loaded with furniture and various other household goods donated by my in-laws. I was pregnant again, this time planned. Motherhood was a powerful responsibility, and hard work, and the strongest human bond I could imagine.

It's about four hundred miles from San Francisco to Ashland, just across the Oregon border. Once we were well out of the Bay Area I was surprised at the open country. We drove on lonely two-lane roads, and the small towns were far apart. After we'd gone at least three hundred miles, there didn't seem to be any towns. I'll relate my reaction to open country by quoting from one of Mike's books, *An Old Man Remembering Birds*: "When we were driving through northern California to Ashland in the late summer of 1966 – there was no interstate freeway then – Hilde broke out crying somewhere south of Yreka. Never in her life had she ever seen so much open country with no trace of civilization anywhere. I did my best to console her, to convince her that she'd adjust."

Perhaps the wilderness we fear is the pause between our own heartbeats, the silence that reminds us we live by grace.

Terry Tempest Williams

BREAD AND CHEESE AND
CHICKEN SALAD

In the summer of 1966, before we left California to establish our home in Ashland, we'd spent two months in Bamberg with my parents. Mike's mother joined us for two weeks and travelled to Berlin and Paris with Mike, and after that took a boat trip from Passau to Vienna on the Danube River with my mother and me while Mike and Pete stayed in Bamberg to practice speaking German with my father.

Beautiful Vienna took us to the heart of European culture. My problem on the boat was an upset stomach I'm sure resulted from my pregnancy. The only minor conflict during our three days in Vienna was when my mother was determined to find a *Kaesebrot* (bread and cheese) for lunch and Mike's mother craved *Haenchen Salat* (chicken salad). We somehow ended up in a restaurant that had neither dish on the menu. There was a strolling violinist there who played "America the Beautiful" for Mike's mother.

Bamberg (population about 80,000), a kind of miniature Vienna, was founded in 902, and Ashland, population about 10,000 when Mike and I arrived, was barely 100 years old. The two places and the people who lived in them didn't have much in common, so southern Oregon was a new world for me, with both pleasant and unsettling surprises.

I knew about Ashland's respected Shakespeare Festival, offering nightly plays in an outdoor theater all summer long. But for the rest of the year it remained an isolated and declining mill town with a small college, 300 miles from Portland and nearly 400 miles from San Francisco. I had doubts and fears about the new environment. At a banquet welcoming new faculty members, the elderly college president spotted a man with a beard who'd come from Alaska among the new hires – and announced in front of everyone that he'd have to shave the beard off before classes started. Hippies hadn't yet arrived in southern Oregon. The only racial minority at the banquet was Japanese-American poet Lawson Inada, who'd been hired to teach creative writing along with Mike. I'm sure I was the only one in the large group with a foreign accent.

I've never had anything against small towns, or what I'd always known as villages. As a child, during and after the war, I'd visited my grandparents, my father's parents, on their farm in the village of Roebersdorf, a few kilometers from Bamberg. Looking back at those days now, I realize that mid-20th century Roebersdorf wasn't all that far removed from the Middle Ages. The village had a town crier who rang his bell every evening and then recited the day's news. To bake their bread, housewives had to carry their loaves to a communal oven near the village square. By far the most popular social event in Roebersdorf was a *Schlachtpartie* (slaughter party). A farmer killed a pig and roasted it whole, and each adult guest was given a knife and fork, bread and mustard, beer, and a plate.

In our new town, for less rent than we'd paid for our San Francisco apartment, we found a comfortable three-bedroom house a short walk from the college campus. Our large back yard had trees, including a giant sequoia, and, through the living room windows, a view across the Rogue Valley to Grizzly Mountain. The nearby countryside – rivers, lakes, mountains - was wild and impressive. Emigrant Lake and the Mount Ashland ski resort were easily accessible from town. People of Ashland were welcoming and friendly, and among the newly hired faculty members were many young men and women, and, counting me, at least three pregnant women among the faculty wives.

Soon after we settled in, deer hunting season opened. I'd already been surprised by the number of pick-up trucks in and around town displaying rifle racks, most of them holding rifles, against their rear windows. On opening day I was surprised again by pick-ups driven by proud hunters displaying dead deer draped over their front fenders. Only the wealthy could afford hunting and fishing privileges in Germany, and the same was true for golf, tennis, and skiing. I decided that I might like the American arrangement better. No place is perfect, or ever will be, and I wanted to adjust.

STOP-AND-GO REELING

In late September Mike started work with afternoon and evening classes on his teaching schedule. He'd taken night classes in San Francisco and chose to teach them because he assumed that so-called nontraditional students – most of them older people who worked at day jobs – signed up for classes because they wanted to, not because they had to accumulate a certain number of credit hours or fulfill an academic requirement.

By mid-October we were settled in and started enjoying our free time. Mike's great-grandfather had taught him to fish on the trout creek that ran through his farmland in western Pennsylvania. After that, in Hawaii in the 1950s, he and his friends spear-fished the coral reefs off Oahu's beaches. Ashland sat between two well known trout, salmon and steelhead rivers, the Rogue, a few miles to our north, and the Klamath, a few miles south across the California border.

Mike had a valid 1966 California fishing license, so we started with the Klamath, the first wild river I'd ever seen up close. In Bamberg I'd observed a few men (and only men) fishing the Regnitz, where there were said to be *Hecht* (pike), but I'd never seen anybody catch one. The river itself was slow-moving, deep and murky, with textile factories spewing foul-looking wastewater into it.

The Klamath was nothing like the Regnitz. On a perfect October Saturday morning, with Mike driving and Pete in back, we made a right turn off the two-lane state highway and drove west on a very lonely road. The river was a series of riffles and whitewater rapids with stretches of calm water between them. Firs and pines grew on the steep slopes of the canyon, and hardwood trees bordering the riverbank had begun to turn, leaves golden in the early light.

About ten miles down the road we parked beside a calm stretch between two riffles. Mike had been told that the fall run of steelhead – seagoing rainbow trout – arrived at the upper Klamath sometime in October, and that the fall run of Chinook salmon would come soon after they did.

"We must be too early," Mike said. "Nobody fishing anywhere. But even if the steelhead aren't here yet there have to be trout around."

While Mike got into his chest waders a single car passed us heading upstream. Coated with dirt from the tires to the windows, it was a sight I'd never seen in Germany. Pete found a handful of small stones and tossed them one by one into shallow water. "Big bird!" he said, pointing with his throwing hand at a heron passing overhead.

Pete and I sat on a flat-topped rock to watch Mike wade in and fish. He used a spinning rod to cast a small silver spoon, or wobbler, out to midstream and beyond, and then retrieve it slowly, taking two steps downstream between casts. Across the river a doe came out of the trees to graze on high green grass under a maple tree. A powerful realization came to me. I loved it here – the sights, the sounds, the smells, the solitude. Since that morning I've never seen a wild river I didn't love.

There were no fish that day, not even a trout, but we drove back to the same place two days later in early morning. Mike waded in farther upstream, and Pete and I sat on the same rock to watch him fish his way toward us. We saw a high-flying V of Canada geese moving westward. Two half-grown deer came out of a willow thicket on the opposite bank, drank from the river, walked slowly downstream and disappeared into a another thicket.

I don't have any idea how much time passed before Mike hooked a steelhead, because, for me, time barely exists on a river. Whatever I'm doing, a pleasurable hour can go by in what seems more like ten minutes. The sounds of moving water – wild water - are hypnotic. I discovered that the sights I see, including small ones that surprise me, and even the ones that should frighten me – a black bear, a nearby rattlesnake - do nothing more or less than make me glad to be where I am. Everywhere else and anything that might be happening there doesn't matter.

I was watching Mike reeling slowly, retrieving the wobbler. The rod suddenly bowed and, simultaneously, at mid-river a big fish jumped high out of water, gleaming even in the shadowed canyon light. Pete and I watched him play, land and release his first steelhead.

***

The weather stayed warm and clear, and every few mornings we drove to the upper Klamath. On a Saturday toward the end of October, dozens of pick-up trucks and trailers were parked wherever there was off-road space for them. After a journey of almost 200 river miles from the Pacific Ocean, the fall Chinook salmon had arrived.

We found a parking space about a hundred yards downstream from our usual spot and then walked back up to watch the action. It had to be a likely place to catch a salmon, because men (and only men), dozens of them, lined the roadside bank, standing no more than a few feet apart, casting baits and lures into the river. Four drift boats had been pulled ashore across from them, and ten or a dozen men were fishing from that side.

When a tall man in a soiled white cowboy hat not far from us hooked a salmon he screamed "Fish on!" at once - an apparent signal for everybody near him to reel in until his fish was either landed or lost. As men on either side of Cowboy Hat reeled in, another "Fish on!" cry came from an elderly man dressed in army camouflage directly across the river, and his friends immediately reeled in too.

Both fishermen, their rods bowed, reeled hard. After a few seconds, Cowboy Hat stopped reeling. "Big one!" he yelled. "Huge!"

Across the river Camouflage was reeling harder than ever. "I bet mine's bigger!" he yelled back.

Then Camouflage stopped, and Cowboy Hat started again, but the stop-and-go reeling didn't last long, because the two of them soon realized they'd hooked and been playing each other. That led to an argument about who should untangle their lines, weights and hooks, and they ended up screaming obscenities back and forth across the river. When Pete asked us what one of the words meant we decided to head home.

We talked about it on the drive home. I told Mike that I was sad about the fact that a crowd of salmon fishermen on a Saturday morning made the Regnitz River in Bamberg look and feel, on this day, like a better place to be than the Klamath.

Nick did not like to fish with other men on the river. Unless they were of your party, they spoiled it.

ERNEST HEMINGWAY, "BIG TWO-HEARTED RIVER"

Mostly warm, dry weather lasted through November, and the Wednesday before Thanksgiving I took Pete to a nearby lake and learned that a single stranger can ruin a fishing day. At an isolated cove, the hook baited with bright red salmon eggs, Pete cast as far as he could into deep water. Then we sat and talked, waiting, hoping, for something to happen. The day was perfect, with the temperature comfortable, a clear blue sky overhead, and a stand of fir trees a few yards behind us. After a while Pete began collecting pieces of driftwood along the shoreline. I stayed sitting beside the propped-up rod, just in case, but nothing happened. When Pete came back to drop off two handfuls of the dry white wood he told me he had to *wisse* – a German child's commonly used equivalent for pee.

I went with him into the fir trees, a few yards behind us. We couldn't have been there more than a minute, and when we came back out of the trees a uniformed state policeman was standing next to the fishing rod. Obviously he'd been hiding somewhere, watching us, waiting for his chance. He wrote out a ticket, charging a visibly pregnant woman, and a five-year-old boy, with "fishing with an unattended pole."

Mike made an official protest and ended up arguing our case in front of a judge and jury. He explained that he understood the clear intent of the regulation – people couldn't be allowed to station five or ten fishing rods at different locations, or to set out baited lines overnight and collect their catch the next morning. Then I recounted exactly what had happened, and how long our pole had supposedly been unattended. In his closing statement, Mike argued the judge into admitting that no law clearly defined what "fishing with an unattended pole" actually meant, and concluded that the decision to cite us had been arbitrary, and for no good reason, and therefore meaningless. The jury of six men and women found us guilty and we paid the fine.

SEVEN POUNDS, EIGHT OUNCES

After hooking a few steelhead with a spinning rod on the Klamath, Mike seriously took up fly-fishing. His great-grandfather had introduced him to the basics of the pastime in Pennsylvania, and now he was learning on his own. The very little I knew about it was what I'd seen during a walk through Golden Gate Park with Mike and Pete not long before we left San Francisco. We'd come upon some men (as always, no women) standing at one end of a rectangular concrete pool waving extra-long fishing rods back and forth, with the visible lines attached to the rods sailing back and then forward over their heads, and finally landing on the water. Mike pointed out the circular floating hoops that served as targets for the flies at the ends of their lines. "We'll both learn how to do it right in Oregon," he said. "They'll have babysitters in Oregon. We'll start not long after our child is born."

I was looking forward to fishing the rivers we visited, even if I'd be one of few women doing it - or especially if I'd be one of the few. In the Germany I grew up in, women's lives were traditionally summarized in three words: *Kinder, Kueche, Kirche* (children, kitchen, church). No matter where I lived, I believed I had a right to want more.

Our child was due in about a week on the warm false spring Saturday morning in late February when Mike was deciding whether or not to drive to the Applegate River, a tributary of the Rogue less than an hour from home.

"I don't think I should go today," he finally said.

We'd made solid arrangements with our neighbors across the street, and we lived no more than ten minutes from the Ashland Hospital. "I already checked with Don and Mary," I said. "They'll be home all day. See if you can catch a steelhead on a fly."

"There's one pool I really want to fish. It's a short walk downstream from the hanging bridge. I'll fish that from top to bottom once. That won't take more than half an hour."

Beginning in early December Mike had fly-fished the Applegate for winter steelhead often, so far without luck. He'd tried in all kinds of weather, from sunny days to snowstorms. He used a cheap fiberglass fly rod, an even cheaper reel, and a secondhand fly line that had cost one dollar at a garage sale. But he didn't blame the equipment. He'd seen other fishermen on the river catch steelhead with bait and lures, and refused to give up.

The date was February 26, 1967, and he hooked a steelhead at the pool below the hanging bridge. He took water into his waders chasing it downstream, and landed it after ten or fifteen minutes. It was his first steelhead on a fly, and, with misgivings, he decided to keep it. On the way home he stopped at the Applegate Store to have it weighed on their butcher's scale. The fish weighed exactly seven pounds, eight ounces.

My labor pains began soon after Mike got home, and that night our daughter Ingrid was born. We named her after my best friend in Germany, and she weighed one ounce more than the steelhead.

***

Four months later we introduced Ingrid to camping. Neither Mike nor I knew much about what we were doing. On so-called camping vacations in Germany, before we had a family car, we'd traveled on my father's motorcycle, with both my parents riding the cycle itself and my brother and me in a sidecar. What Germans called *Zeltplaetze* (tent places) were similar to American parking lots. The orderly spaces were so small that interacting with surrounding families was unavoidable. There was little if any vegetation, and even if a forest was visible in the distance, a town or village was usually closer, often within easy walking distance. Growing up in Hawaii, Mike had never experienced even as much as my so-called camping trips. On the island of Oahu, forty-some miles long and thirty miles wide, there wasn't any logical reason to camp.

We drove south, beyond the Klamath River to California's Scott Valley, a remote historic Gold Rush area. The small, isolated campground we found at the end of a dusty road offered no amenities, not even running water, which might have been why nobody else was there. In mid-afternoon we set up our new tent on a patch of grass in the middle of a dusty clearing. The front tent flap opened to dramatic views of the snow capped Marble Mountains. We furnished the tent with three air mattresses, sleeping bags, an ice chest, a suitcase packed with clothes and necessities, some canned food, and a Coleman stove and lantern. Then, close beside the tent, we set up three folding chairs and the playpen we'd brought for Ingrid.

The day was too hot for comfort, especially inside a canvas tent in the afternoon. Mike went exploring with Pete. We'd told him about the area's history, and he wanted to look for gold. I sat in one of the folding chairs next to Ingrid in her playpen, trying to read. She had toys she usually enjoyed but soon started crying. I thought she might be hungry and lifted her out of the playpen to breast-feed her. Afterwards I carried her into the tent to change her diaper, and in the process she soiled one of the sleeping bags. Then she started crying again, louder than ever. After cleaning up as best I could, I carried her outside and put her back into the playpen. That didn't help, so I went to the car to get her traditional German porcupine doll, *Mecki*, that she slept with every night. I lifted her out of the playpen, lowered her to a patch of grass, and handed *Mecki* to her. She cuddled the doll and sat there smiling up at me.

When I hurried into the tent to check on the sleeping bag I was gone less than thirty seconds, but by the time I came back out Ingrid had managed to crawl a few feet, off the grass and onto fine-grained brown dust. Both Ingrid and *Mecki* were coated with dust, with Ingrid smiling as happily as ever.

I was dirty, sweaty, and miserable. When Mike and Pete got back (without any gold) we packed up and headed home. I bathed Ingrid, and then myself, while Mike heated a can of Dinty Moore beef stew for dinner. All in all, I thought it had been a fairly good day.

––––––––––––––––

In my opinion, camping can be the greatest expression of free will, personal independence, innate ability, and resourcefulness possible today in our industrialized, urbanized existence. Regardless of how miserable or how splendid the circumstances, the sheer experience of camping seems a total justification for doing it.

ANNE LABASTILLE

––––––––––––––––

THE MASSIVE YIELD OF
THE NEW CYCLE

I loved my role as a mother very much. Pete started kindergarten and Ingrid walked and talked. There were other faculty wives with young children, so I had lots of company and made good friends. Our children had playmates, and babysitters were almost always available. I realized that, by American standards, Ashland offered far more than most small towns. In 1967 we saw *Anthony and Cleopatra* and *The Taming of the Shrew* at the Shakespeare Festival. Music from Mozart to country to folk to rock n' roll was presented every summer night at the outdoor Britt Festival in Jacksonville. The college attracted speakers and entertainers from across the country. My favorite singer during those early years was Pete Seeger, in a packed gymnasium, singing songs about environmental issues and the war in Vietnam. The useless and cruel war dragged on, and I joined protests against it whenever I could.

What surrounds any town is at least as important as what happens to be in it, and the southern Rogue Valley is ringed with forested mountains, and lakes and rivers are within easy driving distance. It took me only a few months to learn to fully adapt to solitude in wild country, and I've loved it ever since, in every season of the year.

Richard Nixon has never been one of my favorite people, anyway. For years I've regarded his very existence as a monument to all the rancid genes and broken chromosomes that corrupt the possibilities of the American Dream; he was a foul caricature of himself, a man with no soul, no inner convictions, with the integrity of a hyena and the style of a poison toad. The Nixon I remembered was absolutely humorless. I couldn't imagine him laughing at anything except maybe a paraplegic who wanted to vote Democratic but couldn't quite reach the lever on the voting machine.

HUNTER S. THOMPSON,
THE GREAT SHARK HUNT

Mike had learned about the North Umpqua River from a faculty friend. It was a summer steelhead stream that attracted anglers from almost everywhere. The popularity was based on three factors – the North Umpqua itself was beautiful, and flowed through wild country. It produced large summer steelhead, and thirty miles of the river were restricted to fly-fishing only. In June of 1967, as soon as the spring quarter ended, Mike and an English Department friend drove a hundred miles north on Interstate 5 to the mill town of Roseburg, and then forty miles east on a two-lane road to reach the heart of the fly-fishing water. They fished for two long June days, from before dawn until after dark, and late on the second day Mike finally landed a six-pound summer steelhead. The river soon became an important part of our lives.

Through that summer Mike and I sometimes left the children with a babysitter for an afternoon to fish the Rogue River for rainbow trout at Casey State Park. Wading waist-deep over rocks and boulders in a wild river scared me at first, but Mike helped me when I needed it. When I'd learned to cast reasonably well I began catching trout, first on wet flies, then on dries, and my excitement canceled out my fear.

When we took family camping trips to the Rogue that summer we usually pitched our tent far upstream at Laurelhurst Campground. The river ran through a narrow canyon there, and trout seemed to be everywhere. With Mike's help, Pete caught the first trout of his life. On early mornings and late evenings spring Chinook salmon jumped in the deep pools, and the splats made by the big fish when they hit the water coming down echoed off the canyon walls. Folk music was popular – Joan Baez, Pete Seeger, Bob Dylan – and after dark at Laurelhurst there were usually young men and women sitting around their campfires with guitars, singing songs that actually seemed to mean something. Day or night, listening to songs, or on a blanket near the river, or with her doll *Mecki* in her playpen, Ingrid stayed happy.

Another of our favorite spots on the upper Rogue was MCleod Wayside, several miles downstream from Laurelhurst. It featured a long riffle with a fifty-yard-long island close to the north bank. In October of our second year in Oregon we took Pete and Ingrid there to watch the salmon spawning in the channel between the island and the riverbank.

Most of the spawning fish were spring Chinooks, copper-colored females using their powerful tails to dig their redds (nests) in the gravel streambed, with the darker-colored males nearby, usually behind them, nosing patiently into the current. The largest of the salmon weighed forty pounds or more. Through the summer months they had rested in deep, cool water, and now some of the females were digging their redds in such shallow water that their dorsal fins protruded, so close to the river bank we could have touched them. A few sockeye salmon spawned among the Chinooks, smaller fish, flaming red from their heads to their tails. Not long after spawning, every salmon would die. I was watching a wonder of the world, and I knew it.

Later that year I read a fishing book by Canadian author Roderick Haig-Brown that describes the miracle as well as anybody could:

> *"They come to the spawning gravels in all their brilliant colors – reds, browns, greens, gray, and black and golden. Like the autumn leaves above them, they have their time of fierce glory. Then the frosts and the rains and the winds come. The leaves become torn and sodden and dulled, and in their time they fall, covering the ground, drifting with the stream currents, piling against the rocks and shallows. But within the trees, life is still strong and self-renewing.*

"As the winds stir and drift the dying leaves, so the waters drift and stir the dying salmon against the gray-brown gravels of the stream beds. But under those gravels life is strong and secret and protected in the buried eggs, the real life of the race. Fungus grows on the emptied bodies; they collect in the eddies and strand on the gravel bars, and the bacteria of change work in them to make a new fertility. In spring, life will burst from the gravel as it bursts again from the trees in the massive yield of the new cycle."

BLOOD THAT UNITES
ONE FAMILY

After taking the required class and passing a written exam, I became an American citizen on November 21, 1967. At least twenty of us – from Canada, Mexico, Europe and Africa – said the pledge of allegiance in a ceremony at the Medford Courthouse. Later that month, I failed the driving test in my first attempt to get an American license. I didn't parallel park successfully – I'd never had to park that way in Germany - but after a week of practice I tried again and passed.

During our second full summer in Oregon, Pete and Ingrid were old enough not to merely survive camping trips, but to like them. Out camping, there's no way to make ourselves attractive, much less beautiful. On the last of five days in a tent and sleeping bag I was wearing sweat-stained clothes, my hair was a mess, and I was nearly as dirty as Ingrid had been at the end of our California misadventure. As a joke, I asked Mike how I looked, and he didn't take it as a joke. He stared at me and thought for a while. "You look just fine," he said. "In fact you look wonderful. The thing is, you look real." I knew what he meant.

In the beginning our favorite North Umpqua destination was Island Campground, situated on the river's north bank just above Steamboat Creek. Until I learned the history, that name, Steamboat, always made me wonder. Anyone who sees the creek knows that there never could have been a steamboat anywhere near it, but in the 19th century the creek drainage was seriously prospected for gold. Nobody found much, if any, and back then people who searched hard for gold in places where there wasn't much were said to be "steamboated," thus the name.

Just above its confluence with the North Umpqua the creek featured an ideal swimming hole, complete with sandy beaches backed by old-growth forest. Less than a half-mile downstream from the mouth of the creek was the Steamboat Inn, headquarters for everyone who seriously fly-fished for summer steelhead. We came to know the couple who owned and ran the inn, Frank and Jeanne Moore. Jeanne was a serious botanist and Frank was a D-Day combat veteran, a master angler, a conservationist, and a long-time member of the Oregon Fish and Game Commission.

When the late fall weather turned cold our third year in Oregon we took up cross-country skiing. Pete was old enough to ski, and there were gentle slopes in the Siskiyou Mountains a few miles south of Ashland where the three of us practiced together. Ingrid's first ski trip, in February, happened when we accepted an invitation to join the Moores and their friend Thor, who had a cabin on Diamond Lake, about forty miles upstream from Steamboat Inn. A native of Finland, Thor had cross-country skied for his country in the Winter Olympics, and we stayed overnight at his cabin and spent a day on the slopes of Mount Thielsen with him.

It was a perfect winter day – cold, sunny, fresh powder snow untracked except by birds and animals. We had a mountain to ourselves, but the slopes were steeper than what we were used to, and thick with trees. Mike, Pete and I fell more times than we could count when we tried to add them up at the end of the day. The falls weren't a danger, or even a problem, they were more of an enjoyable joke, on us. Ingrid was the lucky one. She rode down the mountain in Thor's backpack, swerving in and out, quick and smooth among the trees, and, young as she was, she's never forgotten the experience.

For the first time in my life I was beginning to understand how nature actually worked, how everything was related. The snow we enjoyed on Mount Thielsen in February, along with the snow on countless other mountains, would begin melting in March to become the creeks and rivers that nurtured salmon and steelhead runs through the heat of summer.

That night at Thor's cabin we watched a short film titled "Pass Creek" that Frank, with the help of film industry friends from California who fished the North Umqua, had recently produced. It documented the destructive results of clear-cut logging carried out by timber companies. When shade along creeks and rivers was reduced or eliminated by loggers, raised water temperatures killed juvenile salmon, trout and steelhead. Heavy winter storms washed mud and debris from logged-off mountainsides into streams, burying spawning gravel. Frank had his own plane and showed "Pass Creek" all over Oregon and beyond, and it helped pass legislation that still helps protect our rivers.

The earth does not belong to man. Man belongs to the earth. All things are connected like the blood that unites one family. All things are connected. Whatever befalls the earth befalls the sons of the earth. Man did not weave the web of life. He is merely a strand in it. Whatever he does to the web he also does to himself.

CHIEF SEATTLE, 1854

Through our first few years in Oregon we learned about regional environmental issues and, as the children grew, we spent increasing amounts of our free time outdoors. We skied cross-country, and camped, and hunted for mountain quail, and Mike caught steelhead on flies, and I caught trout. During this process I became aware of truths that surprised me. I'd become friends with many of the transplanted Germans who lived in Ashland. None of them, not men or women, young or old, were even remotely interested in any form of outdoor observation or experience. If I'd asked one of them what a steelhead was, they might have guessed some sort of tool, or an automobile part. Mike had told me that growing up in Hawaii he'd come to doubt whether half the people who live on the islands ever so much as set foot on a beach or swim in the Pacific Ocean. I still have no clear idea why so many people have so little motivation or curiosity about understanding our planet, its creatures, and our place among them.

THE FIRST JEWISH-GERMAN
RESTAURANT IN AMERICA

The North Umpqua River watershed became our second home. We eventually discovered Scared Man Campground, three miles up Canton Creek, a Steamboat Creek tributary. In a deep pool not far from Scared Man dozens of steelhead held from early August until fall storms raised the water, allowing them to climb a waterfall and make their way farther upstream to spawn in springtime. We liked to sit with Pete and Ingrid on a rock ledge above the pool and watch the big fish holding under the roily water underneath the falls.

No fishing was allowed in Canton Creek or any other North Umpqua tributary stream. On a hot August day, swimming in the steelhead pool with a facemask, Mike spotted a small silver cylinder wedged between two rocks in deep water. Neither of us had any idea what it might be, and when we took it back to the inn Frank identified it as a blasting cap. He explained that poachers dynamited steelhead pools during low-water summer months. A few years before we'd moved to Oregon, state policemen, thanks to a tip, had arrested three men in a pickup with their truck-bed full of dead steelhead on Canton Creek Road.

Through the summers of 1971 and 1972 Mike and I volunteered to spend our summers working at Steamboat Inn, which was so far from what most people think of as modern life that the inn's phone number at the time was 8F-4. The antique phone itself was operated by a hand crank with communication routed through an unreliable, often unattended Forest Service switchboard. When Mike wanted to check in with his widowed mother in Los Angeles, he had to drive thirty miles downstream to reach a late-twentieth century telephone.

We were forty miles upstream from the town of Roseburg and liked the seclusion, and we wanted to enjoy the river and learn more about it, and possibly, hopefully, eventually help in some way to protect it. Our jobs at the inn were simple. Mike pumped gas, washed dishes, waited on tables, took inexperienced guests fishing, and twice a week drove a van to Roseburg to pick up supplies for the inn. Six cabins behind the inn, on the steep riverbank overlooking the river, accommodated overnight guests. My job was keeping the cabins clean, waiting on tables, and helping in the kitchen. After my first day in the cabins Jeanne went through them to check my work. That night in the kitchen Mildred the cook told me what Jeanne had told her: that I was a genuine German housekeeper for sure, and she wouldn't have to inspect the cabins again. I was tired of the German housekeeper stereotype, but did my best to take it as a compliment. Not long after that, Jeanne told me to my face that an attractive woman with a foreign accent gave the inn class. That wasn't so bad.

The inn operated seven days a week, from 7:30 a.m. (when Mike hung the "Sorry, We're Open" sign on the front window) until at least eleven o'clock at night. The dining room featured a hand-hewn sugar pine table six inches thick and close to thirty feet long, with conventional tables-for-four surrounding it. On one side of the dining room was the kitchen, on the opposite side the door to the Moores' living quarters. Frank and Jeanne had two grown sons, Frankie and Dennis, and a daughter named Colleen, who had been born the same day Pete was.

For road traffic - campers, log-truck drivers, tourists headed to Crater Lake - there were a few shelves of groceries on the kitchen side of the dining room next to a cooler full of soft drinks and beer. Near the back door that led down to the cabins was a counter featuring an assortment of fly-fishing gear – waders, boots, leaders, lines, and both steelhead flies and fly-tying materials, along with a small table with a fly-tying vise attached for anyone who wanted to use it. Pete began learning to tie flies over the course of our first summer. The inn stayed open to the general public until six p.m., when the kitchen crew began preparing the "fishermen's dinner," served long after dark, due to the fact that legal fishing time lasted until one hour after sunset.

Besides cabin guests, campers and residents of Roseburg often made dinner reservations. Every night the long table was full, and usually the smaller tables too. The food was well prepared and reasonably priced, and on the busiest nights we had as many as fifty guests. I cooked sauerbraten for everybody several times through the summer.

I'd always enjoyed cooking, and had even been offered a partnership in a restaurant that a young Jewish friend from New York planned on opening in Ashland. In making his offer, Henry told me he was certain our enterprise would become the first Jewish-German restaurant in America. I liked the idea but turned the offer down, and no restaurant ever happened because Henry moved to Canada to avoid the possibility of being drafted and sent to Vietnam.

Mike and I weren't paid for our work. The agreement was that Mike would be free to fish the river every summer evening until dark, and I had afternoons off to spend time with Pete and Ingrid at the Steamboat Creek swimming hole. Some of our friends in Ashland wondered out loud why we'd be willing to do such work without pay (or even with it), and I was sure that some of the friends who kept quiet were being polite.

"Bumming around the country" as he put it, Mike had done menial work and came to believe that everybody, even rich kids, or especially rich kids, should have to do enough common labor to understand what it's like and why it's necessary, and to realize that many fine people, through little or no fault of their own, have to do such work through much or all of their lives. I have a related thought that I normally keep to myself. I've known many professors and liked almost all of them, but quite a few have been in school nearly all their lives, from kindergarten through graduate school and then as members of a faculty. Can they truly understand what life on earth is like for most people?

The starlings in front of my window continually display their art: they can sound like orioles, quails, corncrakes, even frogs, but they haven't a voice of their own. I call them professors.

LEO TOLSTOY, IN A LETTER

I CAN'T HARDLY TURN
THE DAMN WHEEL

Soon after we started work Mike had the first of two encounters he's never forgotten, both involving education. The first happened when he was filling the gas tank of an overdressed middle-aged man's big late model car. The tourist mentioned he was on his way to Crater Lake, and as Mike cleaned his front windshield, he stuck his head out. "Thanks," he said. "No offense, but if you got a formal education you wouldn't have to do work like this. There's probably still time for you. No offense at all, young man, but you should think about it." Mike was an assistant professor and published writer by then, and kept it to himself.

We lived in a small trailer not far from the inn's guest cabins. Pete and Ingrid slept in the Moores' quarters, where there was plenty of space. When we moved into the trailer we immediately discovered a dead cat, probably killed by a raccoon. The unlucky animal was easy to dispose of, and the trailer aired out after two or three hours. Another incident involving our trailer happened our first night there. When Mike got into the double bed, before I got in with him, one of the legs broke, so we spent the night sleeping at an angle. Early the next morning Frank broke out laughing when Mike told him about the broken bed. "I wish I was young again," he said, and the story circulated around the inn for days.

The only paid help at Steamboat Inn was Mildred, who supervised preparation of the late evening fishermen's dinners. She was a heavyset, middle-aged blond who liked her work, and did it well, and had a sense of humor. I was in the kitchen when Jeanne tried to convince Mildred she could improve her health by taking vitamin C.

"I'm way ahead of you," Mildred said. She reached under the table she was working at and lifted out a bottle of Canadian Club. "I already take vitamin CC."

Another time, when Jeanne and I were helping her with dinner, she held up a badly wilted stalk of celery. "Look at this," she said with a smile. "Like a ninety-year-old man."

Inn guests included doctors, lawyers, businessmen, policemen, professors, teachers, occasional so-called fishing bums too, and even a few politicians, including Oregon's governor, Tom McCall. A Dan Callaghan photo of the governor with a steelhead he landed at the Kitchen Pool eventually became a ten-foot tall statue, created by Rip Caswell and placed in Riverfront Park in Salem. Some famous literary names appeared at the inn while Mike and I were there, including Jack Hemingway, son of Ernest, and Loren Grey, son of Zane.

On a relatively slow night in the kitchen Mildred told a story about Loren Grey in the old days, when the only access to the Steamboat Creek area was the narrow dirt road high above the river's north bank. A younger Mildred had fished the North Umpqua, and was driving downstream toward Roseburg when Loren Grey and a friend came around a bend, heading upstream. One vehicle would have to back up a considerable distance to allow the other to pass. Loren immediately ordered Mildred to back up, and she immediately refused. After a standoff that lasted at least an hour, Loren finally gave in and backed up a long way, giving Mildred the room she needed to get by. "He was a goddamn spoiled brat," Mildred said. "Everybody around here knew that. He used to go so far as to hire stooges to stand knee-deep in the water from the crack of dawn on at the spots he wanted to fish, to keep everybody else out until he got there. I sure as hell didn't see him as anybody who could tell me what to do."

Dan Callaghan, a lawyer from Salem, was a master of both photography and fly-fishing. He told me a story about his friend Jack Hemingway, who came up the old dirt road to fish the river with a friend shortly after World War Two ended. There wasn't so much as a dirt road above Steamboat Creek then, so the two men fought their way up the north bank through old-growth forest, fishing with ultra-light trout gear as they went. Instead of the trout they expected to catch they hooked steelhead, but with their light trout gear they didn't land a single fish.

Through June, July and August the inn was always full – reservations were often made months in advance – and guests checked in and out through the summer. There were families with children, married couples without them, young and old, city people and country people, occasional foreigners, and a few braggarts (usually about fishing) – but for those of us who worked there the schedule varied little from day to day.

Frank was in the kitchen ready to cook breakfasts by seven o'clock, and Mike was ready to wait on tables, serve meals, wash dishes, make sure there was always coffee available, pump gas out front, and work the cash register. Guests at the inn who fished had been out on the river for at least an hour and a half by 7:30, and guests who didn't fish were normally still in bed. Most of the early breakfast customers were log truck drivers and timber workers who traveled in large vans known as "crummies" on their way to the woods.

Hippies had reached Southern Oregon by the 1970s, and Frank was glad to let one or two or three of them sweep the parking lot, whether it needed sweeping or not, in exchange for big breakfasts afterwards. The busiest mornings came when a full busload of tourists on their way to Crater Lake stopped for breakfast. With everything happening at once Frank and Mike worked hard, and Frank paid a price. Cooking ten or more breakfasts at a time, over-easy eggs didn't always come out perfectly, and he shoved the rejects to the edge of the grill and started over with two more eggs. He hated wasting anything, so late in the morning, after Jeanne and I started work, he ate the rejected eggs – as many as a dozen at a time.

Mike described the busiest mornings as borderline chaos. In the beginning I saw almost everything in and around the inn as a form of chaos, because for all my life in Germany just about everything had been *planmaessig* (organized and on time). If a train or bus was scheduled to either arrive or depart at 10:37 a.m. or p.m., it did exactly that. Every Saturday morning we cleaned and shined our shoes whether they needed it or not. When the car was in our garage we locked the garage, even when we were home. Whatever we ordered to be delivered to the house – cases of wine and beer, charcoal briquettes for the stoves that provided heat – arrived within a few minutes of the scheduled time. Above all else, everything, inside and out, was neat and orderly. Clothes were never thrown over the backs of chairs and dirty dishes weren't left in the sink. Washed clothes were taken off clotheslines as soon as they were dry, and in wintertime snow was shoveled off the driveway and the sidewalk out front a few minutes after snow had stopped falling.

Frank's shed, out front near the gas pumps, came nowhere near meeting the standards I grew up with. The place was a conventional German's nightmare. Frank had built Steamboat Inn and the cabins and shed himself, in the early 1950s, and tools he had used then took up at least half the shed's floor space. All four walls were piled to the ceiling with what, to me, looked like junk – large and small hunks of wood, rolls of rusty wire, coffee cans full of bent nails, nuts, bolts and screws, other cans containing what I thought might be worn out auto parts. Scattered around randomly were rat traps, ax-heads and saws without handles, worn shingles, lengths of rope, bedsprings, buckets with holes in them, bushel baskets of unidentifiable objects, dirty glass jars, torn rubber boots.

I wasn't the only one who noticed the shed and its contents. One morning I overheard two guests, fishermen from the San Francisco Bay Area having late after-fishing breakfasts, talking about it.

"I check that shed out every year, the first day I get here," one of them said. "I told Frank I'd gladly pay to have the place cleaned out and cleaned up."

"That's a reasonable idea. There's no more room for anymore junk in there, that's for sure. So what'd Frank say?"

"No thanks is what he said. He said you never can tell when somebody might need something he's got in there."

No more than a week later a tall, slim, glum looking log truck driver came into the inn while Jeanne was in the kitchen, I was having an early lunch, Mike was washing dishes, and Frank was straightening out the fly fishing products behind the glass counter near the back door.

"I'm in serious trouble, Frank," the driver said. "I was damn lucky to make it this far. All of a sudden, right before I got to Island Campground, my steering went bad. I can't hardly turn the damn wheel. I'm lucky I *made* it here. An' I got a perfect six-log load out there headed for the mill. You got any ideas? At least you got a phone."

"Let's take a look," Frank said, and they walked out the front door together.

I watched through the front window while I ate. Both men looked under the hood from both sides of the truck. After a minute or two, Frank walked across the parking lot and into the shed, and a few minutes later came back out with a small metal object in his hand. Approaching the driver, he held up whatever it was and smiled. Ten minutes later the log truck pulled out of the lot, heading for the Roseburg mill.

———————————

To keep every cog and wheel is the first precaution of intelligent tinkering.

ALDO LEOPOLD

———————————

RIGOR AND MORTIS

In late June two teenage California boys arrived to spend the summer in a small ramshackle trailer out back not far from the one Mike and I were housed in. They were the sons of two old friends of Frank who stayed at the inn every year for a week of fishing in mid-August. The plan was for their sons to do odd jobs and help around the inn to earn their room and board, and fish in their ample free time, and then travel back home with their fathers in August. I can't remember their first names, because Mildred gave them nicknames not long after they arrived – Rigor and Mortis. They were good kids who laughed at the joke along with everybody else, and as far as work went they happily did whatever they were asked to do.

Soon after Rigor and Mortis joined the Steamboat Inn crew, Mike took me fishing to what was called the Camp Water, with Pete and Ingrid at the children's dinner prepared by Mildred and Jeanne, and Mortis covering for me in the kitchen. The Camp Water begins just above the mouth of Steamboat Creek and ends not far above the Inn. The name goes back to a man named Clarence Gordon, who had established a tent camp for anglers soon after World War Two. North Umpqua steelhead hold in the same spots year after year, and nearly every place they hold has a name. The Camp Water begins with the Surveyor

Pool, just above Steamboat Creek. From Surveyor down to the inn, these are the names that everyone who seriously fishes the river knows well: Surveyor; Hayden Run; Sweetheart; Station; Upper Boat; Lower Boat; Upper Kitchen; Kitchen; Fighting Hole; Upper Mott; Middle Mott; Lower Mott. Mike had landed his first North Umpqua steelhead at the Lower Boat Pool, named that because before Mott Bridge was built the water there was calm enough for anglers to use a rowboat to cross the river and reach Clarence Gordon's camp.

The place Mike took me to fish was the Kitchen Pool, where, in the old days, Gordon's kitchen tent had been located on the south riverbank. On a warm evening in June we drove across Mott Bridge, parked in the Forest Service lot, and walked down the steep trail to the river.

"We timed it right," Mike said. "The sun'll be off the water in fifteen or twenty minutes."

Not many steelhead had reached the Camp Water yet, so fishing had been slow and the river wasn't crowded. There was an angler at the Station Pool near the mouth of Steamboat Creek, another at the Upper Boat pool, and one more at the Middle Mott, well below the Kitchen.

We were in chest waders and customized Vietnam combat boots with snow tire studs driven into the rubber soles to give traction on the river's slippery bedrock. When we waded out Mike carried my fly rod, with a black and white Skunk fly tied to the tippet of an eight-pound-test leader. I wasn't quite frightened, but I was uneasy. Our destination was a ledge near the middle of the river, and to get there I'd have to cross a channel at least four feet deep.

Mike, upstream to my right, held my right hand in his free left hand as we started out across the gravel bottom. "It's not as bad as it looks," he said. By the time we were thigh-deep the current felt surprisingly strong. We stopped at the edge of the drop-off into the channel. When Mike hopped down the water reached well above his waist. When he reached for my hand I wasn't sure I wanted to do it, and he saw it on my face.

"Come on now. The water's pretty high but you'll be fine."

When I hopped down I realized I was standing near the middle of a wild river, the current pushing hard. Before I had time to worry about it, Mike had quickly climbed onto the ledge and pulled me up behind him. The ledge surface was nearly flat and barely a foot deep. A few feet in front of us was a wide, deep, channel - the Kitchen Pool. "We'll wade up to the top and then fish our way down to the rapids."

As we waded up the ledge Mike explained things to me. "When the fish come up through rapids they like to hold where the water deepens and slows. In the Kitchen they usually hold at the lower end, but it's possible to hook one anywhere. So we'll work our way down from the top."

That was what we did. Another underwater ledge like the one we stood on was straight across from us, no more than thirty feet away. Mike stood to my left as I made my first short casts, straight across-stream toward the ledge. Just after my line landed on the smooth surface I made an upstream mend to slow the fly down. The Skunk, a few inches deep, swung slowly across the pool. When I had enough line out to cover the water all the way to the op-posite ledge, I began taking a step downstream between casts.

"Relax," Mike said. "Keep making nice straight casts and then a mend. If a fish hits you'll know it. It'll probably run downstream, maybe out of the pool into the rapids, down into the Mott. You can't stop it so don't touch your reel if it runs."

During fishermen's dinners I'd heard guests talk about going days without a steelhead, or even so much as a missed strike or a fish rising to the surface but not touching the fly. Even in the best years fishing was rela-tively slow in June, but the early steelhead that arrived, not very long out of the ocean, were the brightest, strongest fish of the year. I couldn't believe I'd hook one, and wasn't quite sure I really wanted to.

"It's not an easy river," Mike said, "you know that. But it's not as bad as it seems at first. You'll get used to wad-ing it. You'll get to where you feel comfortable. And if you ever fall in, the main thing is, don't panic. You've heard the myth I think – the one about how if your waders fill up with water you'll sink and drown. But that's pure bull-shit. The water inside your waders doesn't weigh any more than the water outside. So if you ever do fall into fast wa-ter, any kind of water – and maybe you won't, but if you do – just stay calm and tread water facing downstream with your feet out in front of you and grab the first convenient dry rock you come to. You're a good swimmer. There's al-ways a nearby place to wade out. Stay calm, that's the main thing. I'll be with you anyway, always. Look. Somebody stopped up there to watch you fish."

When I looked I saw a car parked high on the opposite bank alongside the road, and a dark-haired woman was watching us through the driver's side window. She was in sunlight and now we were in shade. A few casts later, not quite halfway down the pool, the fly stopped near midstream. For a second I thought I might be snagged on a rock. It had happened to me trout fishing. Then the weight increased and line tore from the reel. At the tail of the pool a writhing fish jumped high and landed and immediately jumped again.

The woman parked across the road honked her horn.

"He's coming upstream now!" Mike said. "Reel until the line's tight!"

"I'll never land it!" I said.

"You will!"

Mike sounded nervous now, and I was well beyond that. Aside from his advice, hearing the car horn was the last clear and certain memory I have. All sense of time was gone. It seemed to me a miracle had happened. The steelhead ran up and down the Kitchen Pool and jumped twice or three or four times more, and I know Mike told me what to do, and I must have done it.

After I have no idea how long, I saw the played-out steelhead through the water, shiny silver, with a faint pink lateral line, and the white wing of the Skunk fly visible in the upper lip, and the leader angling at a tangent through the clear water.

"Hatchery fish have clipped fins," Mike said. "This one's a beautiful native female. Keep the line tight and the rod tip high and take two steps back, there's plenty of room."

Mike knelt on the ledge, reached down, and lifted the steelhead out of water with one hand by the wrist of her tail. With his other hand he slid the barbless hook from her lip.

"Watch," he said.

When I stepped to the edge of the ledge he lowered the fish into the river, still gripping the wrist of the tail, and held her facing into the current. After a few seconds he released his grip and she surged away, tail pumping, and then suddenly turned for the bottom and disappeared. The woman watching from her car honked again and waved, and after I waved back she drove away.

"Some people think it's cruel to land fish and release them," Mike said. "That you're torturing innocent creatures for no reason. The way I see it, we're educating the fish we release. The next time they see a fly, one that belongs to somebody who'd kill them, they might know enough to ignore it."

I was too excited to think about anything. I don't remember wading out of the river and walking back to the car. I do remember that nearly everyone at the fishermen's dinner congratulated me. I still had a hard time believing I'd landed a steelhead in a river that was widely known as the graduate school of steelhead fly-fishing.

A few hours later, when I woke up in the middle of the night, I understood that I'd been attached to something wild and elemental, and in my mind I saw my first steel-head surging toward the river bottom, disappearing back to where she belonged.

fishing the North Umpqua

With summer life at the inn constantly changing, it was always interesting. Day after day, week after week, fishing families and fishing buddies from all over the country came and went. Nearly all of them were nice people. During conversations before, during and after the late dinners I noticed what I saw as a satisfying contrast. Most of the men, along with many of their wives, were professional people who lived in cities. In both Germany and America these were people who at social gatherings did a lot of talking about their occupations, and when meeting someone new one of the first questions they were sure to ask was, "What do you do?" At Steamboat Inn guests talked about the river, the surrounding forests, hiking trails, birds and animals, wild flowers, steelhead fishing, and the interrelated conservation issues that mattered. They were people glad to be exactly where they were.

Nature we have always with us, an inexhaustible storehouse of that which moves the heart, appeals to the mind, and fires the imagination – health to the body, a stimulus to the intellect, and joy to the soul. The born naturalist is one of the most lucky men in the world. Winter or summer, rain or shine, at home or abroad, walking or riding, his pleasures are always at hand. The great book of nature is open before him and he has only to turn its leaves.

JOHN BURROUGHS

But a few of the men were what I knew as *Angebers* in German. In America they're called braggarts. The ones who leered at me in embarrassing ways were easy to ignore. The most amusing braggarts were the ones who flew to San Francisco and rented cars to drive from the airport to Steamboat Inn, a distance of close to 500 miles. Driving at a reasonable speed in normal traffic the trip should take something close to nine hours, but these men boasted about getting all the way from the San Francisco airport to the inn in as little as six hours, which would have meant driving well over 80 miles per hour without stopping anywhere along the way. Why would anybody tell such a lie? What was the point? I've been wondering about it for more than a half century and still don't know, and never will.

Mike took the summer's most obnoxious braggart fishing one evening, and, forty-five years later, he finally wrote a *High Country News* article about it. I have the author's permission to quote part of it here:

… I have vivid memories of one of the guests I dealt with. He was a real estate developer from New York City with reddish blond hair and a bland face with a single distinctive characteristic: a protruding mouth that resembled that of a fish, which made it look like he could have picked objects off a tabletop using only his lips.

In the dining room at lunchtime when we made our fishing plans, he showed me a photo of the opulent interior of his Manhattan Home. (Mike described the photo as looking like a Mel Brooks representation of a French brothel, but an editor deleted the sentence before publication). *That evening, as we left the inn in my car, he began bragging about huge fish he had caught in other places.*

"All I need here's one big steelhead, on a picture. I got pictures of damn near everything I ever killed. And believe me, I'm a good fisherman. Very good! You'll see. Very, very good!"

When I tried to explain some of the basics to him, he cut me off: "If I toss a fly in the river I don't see why a steelhead won't eat my damn fly as fast as anybody else's, right? It's mostly luck, right? Well I'm lucky! Smart too! Hey! That blond who helps serve meals is a gorgeous broad."

"Yes she is," I agreed.

"'You made a move on her yet?"

"'She's my wife."

"'You might be lucky I'm leaving tomorrow. Got to get back and work on my deals, big deals. Believe me, you are lucky. Very, very lucky."

I changed the subject by asking him if he'd ever fished for steelhead before.

"Once. Tried that Klamath River right down south in California. The thing I couldn't understand was, the place we fished was 200 miles from the ocean, and my guide tells me there aren't any dams from where we were all the way to the ocean. What the hell's that all about? All that good water going to waste! Look around here! How come there's nothing anywhere? Develop! That's exactly what I do in New York. Ever been to New York? Manhattan, I mean?"

"I worked in Macy's shoe department once."

"In Manhattan?"

"Yes."

"'What'd you do at Macy's?"

"I was in the shoe department stockroom."

"And look at you now, stuck out here in the boondocks. Should've got an education maybe, huh?"

The first spot we tried was a relatively easy one, where an angler could stand high on a streamside boulder with a clear back-cast, and the steelhead, if any happened to be holding in the pool, would be about 10 feet out and 30 feet downstream. I helped the developer up onto the boulder – he nearly fell twice – and gave him directions. "See the underwater rock?" I pointed.

"Yeah, yeah."

"Just try to bring your fly across right behind the rock."

As a fly angler, on a scale of 1 to 10 the developer was a minus 2 or 3. I drove him from pool to pool until dark without a result. Given his skill level, and if he was as lucky as he claimed to be, it would likely have taken him a month or more of hard fishing to hook a steelhead. He cursed the river, and me, all the way back to the lodge.

The last time I saw him was the following morning. Hilde and I watched from a kitchen window while he had his picture taken, posing with a 10-pound steelhead that another guest had caught and stored in the cooler. After the photo shoot, the developer drove away alone in an expensive car, while the gorgeous broad and I went back to work.

***

No insect hangs its nest on threads as frail as those which will sustain the weight of human vanity.

EDITH WHARTON

BEER, WINE, BOURBON, SCOTCH, GIN

Through July and August the many public camp-grounds both up and downstream from the inn were full, and road traffic had at least doubled since June. In 1971, a better than average run of steelhead had attracted more anglers than usual. Mid-morning and mid-afternoon were the relatively slow times at the inn, and I took Pete and Ingrid to the Steamboat Creek swimming hole, usually with families and their children who were guests at the inn. Pete was nine years old, Ingrid four. On rare days when I was especially busy with cabins the kids went without me, cared for either by helpful guests or families from the Forest Service camp across the river.

Ingrid became a fine swimmer for her age. When she and Pete had had enough swimming, they spent their time catching crawdads in shallow water, depositing them in a small pool at the creek's edge, and then putting them back where they came from when it was time to leave.

There were almost always children at the inn, tempo-rary playmates for them, sometimes only one or two, often a half dozen or more. Ingrid, never shy, learned to wait on log truck drivers who wanted coffee, and who always gave her a tip when she came to the table to carry their empty cups to the kitchen. Pete, who loved hamburgers, had one for lunch every day for three months. His summer fishing highlight was the evening Mike took him out to the Fighting Hole, the small steelhead pool just below the Kitchen. They waded out, Mike hooked a steelhead, and let Pete play it for ten minutes and land and release it.

After my June steelhead at the Kitchen Pool, another fishing highlight happened on an evening in July. When Pete and Ingrid were in the inn's backyard with playmates, Mike drove us about five miles downstream to the Fairview Pool, a deep, narrow run of water between two dry ledges. I'd never fished there before, and Mike walked me up to the top of the roadside ledge, pointing out places where steelhead might be holding. Then he left me alone to fish and walked downstream and around a bend to a little known pool called Chet's Run. He was wearing waders and I wasn't, because I could fish Fairview without getting my feet wet.

I worked my way down the pool the standard way, watching my Skunk land and sink close to the opposite ledge, mending my floating line, watching the line swing across the deep pool, then finally taking a long step downstream to cast again. It was as easy as North Umqua fly fishing gets, standing high and dry with a clear back-cast. I'd hooked and landed five or six steelhead by then, all of them at the Camp Water, and each had come as a wonderful surprise. I liked it that way, not really expecting anything. For me, simply enjoying the river's sights and sounds served as an effective form of meditation.

At the tail of Fairview the current narrowed and gathered speed to form a V that fed into a churning white-water rapids. A round-topped underwater rock that Mike had pointed out as a likely place to raise a steelhead was visible just above the V on the far side. I made a good cast there, dropping the fly to the far side of the rock and mending the line. Just after the mend, the line stopped. I felt a sudden, heavy weight and, as I had when I hooked my Kitchen fish, thought I'd snagged the fly on the rock. I raised the rod tip, hoping to yank it free, and then saw an underwater silver flash close to where I thought my fly should be.

Line rushed from the reel as the hooked steelhead ran down the V into the rapids. My fly line was ninety feet long and the old Hardy reel I used held more than a hundred yards of nylon backing behind the fly line. When I looked at the reel the fly line was long gone and backing was peeling away. The Hardy made a screaming mechanical noise and the handle spun in a blur. I hurried as fast as I could safely go to the bottom edge of the ledge. By then more than half the backing was gone. Far downstream I saw the steelhead jump high and hang in the air and fall. For a second or two the reel stopped spinning, and then it started again, screaming louder than ever.

If I wanted any chance to land the fish I'd have to follow it downstream, but I couldn't do that with my line on the river side of the huge boulder blocking my way. I raised the rod tip as high as I could reach to try to get the tight-stretched nylon backing over the boulder. I couldn't reach quite high enough. I inched my way closer to the river. The water forcing its way through the V made a loud roar. The rod tip was close, the backing inches from clearing the boulder, and then, standing on tip-toe, my right hand braced against the boulder, I lost my balance and fell face-first into the river.

Later, Mike told me what he saw on his way upstream from Chet's Run - my arm sticking up out of the water, my hand holding my fly rod high. By the time he reached me I'd made it onto the rocky bank where the water slows in the widened river between Fairview and Chet's Run.

What I remember about the experience is that after falling in, the roar of the river was much louder than ever, and I had no control over my body. With my eyes open all I saw was green light.

Suddenly I found myself standing on the riverbank beside my husband, wet and cold, wondering how I got there. My first words were, "What happened?"

"I saw you climbing out of the river!" Mike said.

"I'm all right," I said. "I hooked a fish and fell in."

"What?"

"I hooked a fish and fell in."

"Reel in your line."

"What?"

"Reel in your line."

"Why?"

"Do you want me to do it? Are you really okay?"

"No."

"You're not okay?"

"I don't want you to do it."

"Then do it, okay? I can tell by your line that the steelhead's still on."

I tried to believe it, and I reeled as fast as I could. It took a long time to recover the backing and then the fly line. When the line was finally tight the steelhead made another downstream run.

Mike and I followed after the fish as fast as we could, stepping around and over rocks, and I reeled as we went to keep the line tight. I could feel the life of the steelhead through the line and fly rod all the way to Chet's Run, where it had stopped to hold down deep against the bottom. The fish was played out, and I knew what to do. I reeled slowly and steadily, one turn at a time, lifting, working it off the bottom, looking for it through the water.

"There!" I said when I saw it.

"Back up slow, one step at a time."

I took three or four careful steps back, and Mike, at the water's edge, reached out to take my leader in his hand. He held it and slowly lifted, hand over hand. The fish was no more than a foot underwater when he slid his hand down the leader to twist the Skunk from its upper lip. This was a male fish with a dark red lateral line, and it drifted a few feet downstream, then seemed to realize it was free, and pumped its tail and surged back up to hold exactly where it had been released, clearly visible again, steady in the current.

"Twelve pounds," Mike said. "At least twelve. A native male. And he'll be fine."

It seemed as if the steelhead overheard. Yes, he was fine, and I was glad to watch him drift downward toward midstream and then suddenly disappear.

Back at the inn there were two loggers' crummies and five or six cars in the parking lot. The first thing I did after Mike dropped me off was change into dry clothes in our trailer. Then, without taking time to comb my hair, I checked on Pete and Ingrid, still playing with friends in the backyard. When I walked into the kitchen Mildred was smiling. "You caught one," she said.

"How could you tell?"

"I could tell as soon as I saw you get out of the car. I could tell by the look on your face. And you were soaking wet too. Where was it?"

"Fairview!"

"Did you jump in or fall in?"

I was tempted to lie, but didn't. "Fell," I said.

"Be careful out there."

"I will be. I was careful. But I fell anyway and made it back out."

"How big was the fish?"

"At least twelve pounds."

"Oh my God. No wonder you're excited. Frank took Nat out to the Camp Water. Go see if Rigor and Mortis need help in the dining room. I'm fine here, for now."

Nat Reed was a guest from Florida, and the assistant secretary of the interior for fish, wildlife and national parks, who was stopping at the inn for three nights.

In the dining room the boys were handling loggers drinking after-work beers and customers off the road with coffee and milkshakes, hamburgers and chili dogs. On my way back into the kitchen I couldn't help but notice one of the loggers, beer in hand, staring at me.

After the late dinner I helped Rigor and Mortis carry plates, dishes and silverware into the kitchen, where Mike was stationed at the dishwasher. As an enlisted man in the army he'd been well trained for that work, where on KP (Kitchen Patrol) duty he'd sometimes washed the pots, pans, dishes and silverware utilized by cooks and 200 enlisted men at a time in the battalion mess hall

But the inn was nothing like a mess hall. Every night after dinner, many guests sat at the long sugar-pine table to talk and trade stories, and sip beer, wine, bourbon, Scotch, gin. The long table itself and the people who sat there socializing reminded me of the tables where Mike and I had sat drinking smoked beer and talking with strangers at the Schlenkerla in Bamberg.

No anglers ever got close to drunk, because they'd be back out on the river long before dawn. All summer long, I never heard a serious after dinner argument. Mike and I knew that most of the guests were Republicans, and we weren't, but it never came close to becoming an issue. There were more important things to talk about: where the steelhead were holding as the river gradually lowered and the water temperature steadily rose; which flies, and what size, were attracting strikes; whether the water was low enough for dry flies to work; the fact, as all experienced anglers saw it, that the hatchery fish the state was dumping into the river to supplement dwindling native runs were inferior creatures. Could anything be done about it beyond killing the hatchery fish that we landed? Usually there was a lighter conversational side too. Recipes were traded, jokes and stories told, and I remember a special night when a well known folk singer came to dinner and performed for us, and invited everyone to join in, and the singing didn't stop until after midnight.

On the night of the Fairview steelhead I sat near one end of the big sugar pine table, relaxing with a glass of white wine across from a husband and wife from the Bay Area. Mike, with a bottle of beer, joined us after the dishes were done. When he told the couple I'd landed a steelhead, they wanted me to tell them all about it, and I did. I tried not to brag, but I admit to liking the attention. With luck, I'd managed to do something difficult well.

I fished with Mike fairly often through the summer, and landed and released a dozen or more steelhead. After the Fairview experience, for reasons I don't understand, the river didn't scare me. If anything, I became overconfident. Waist-deep in a pool on the upper river, I waded one step too far and suddenly found myself swimming. I hung onto my rod and stumbled ashore downstream, and kept fishing. At Fall Creek, standing on a slippery underwater rock, I took a careless step when I saw a steelhead jump downstream, and suddenly I was underwater. This time I dropped my fly rod, but I was lucky. When I made it ashore I saw the rod stranded against a downstream rock in a place I could easily reach.

Mike and I, and Pete and Ingrid, were sorry to leave the inn and drive home after Labor Day weekend. We'd already decided to work there for another summer, and after that we'd be leaving for a sabbatical year in Bamberg.

***

Our lives in Ashland settled into a pattern unlike anything I could ever have imagined in Bamberg. Mike's afternoon and evening classes left his mornings free to write, and he never taught summer school. The free time was much too valuable to waste making a little more money. On many fall weekends we camped with Pete and Ingrid, and there was usually enough snow to cross-country ski by early December. Once on a December night Mike and I skied under a bright full moon. We made a long downhill run on a logging road through second-growth trees. A pack of coyotes followed us most of the way, howling in the night. They stayed close, but hidden by trees, and we never saw them. It could have been the moon that made them howl long and loud that way, or the sound of our skis hissing through powder snow. Whatever made it happen, that was a special night.

I practiced fly casting in our backyard in any weather, and Mike tied trout and steelhead flies. We socialized with faculty friends, town friends, and some of Mike's students, including Africans from Kenya, Uganda and Nigeria who rented rooms not far from our home. I spent time with my German clique of friends, mostly women who, like me, had come to America as young women.

We watched plays at the Shakespeare Festival, and listened to music at the Britt Festival in Jacksonville. Mike's parents came to visit fairly often, and we visited them in San Francisco. We still enjoyed the city – the restaurants, Golden Gate Park, the art museums, especially the De Young and the Legion of Honor. But I realized that even though I found satisfaction in cities, I didn't miss the cities after I was gone.

IT LOOKS LIKE A
POTATO DUMPLING

The second summer at Steamboat Inn was, if anything, better than the first. Because we knew them, our summer jobs seemed easier. Many of the inn's guests who returned year after year were happy to see us again, and we were glad to see them. Pete and Ingrid reconnected with children they knew. The run of fish was above average again, and Pete, at age 10, began seriously fishing for steelhead. Mike was always with him, but he hooked and landed fish on his own.

On an early August evening Dan Callaghan – the angler, lawyer, professional photographer, and recent appointee to the Oregon Fish and Game Commission – waded across the river with his camera to take photos of Pete fishing the Station Pool just below the mouth of Steamboat Creek. Hopefully, his photographs would accompany an article Mike was writing for an outdoor magazine. The theme was that an argument commonly made against fly-fishing only restrictions - that it wasn't fair to exclude children - wasn't valid.

The near-miracle happened. Not long after Mike had helped Pete across the river to the pool, he hooked and played a steelhead. The fish ran downstream all the way to the Lower Boat Pool. Mike helped Pete follow it down, and Dan ended up with a series of excellent photos that proved a ten-year old could hook a steelhead with a fly rod on a very challenging river.

Some of my happiest fishing experiences that summer were the times I hooked fish when male anglers happened to be watching. Usually when that happened, it was easy to see that they were surprised, and at least jealous if not angry. One evening at Jeanne's Pool, on the road side of the river not far below the inn, I landed and released a fish while a middle-aged man in waders watched everything from the trail side, straight across the river. He wasn't a guest at the inn or anyone I'd ever seen before. After I released the fish I smiled and waved. His acknowledgment was to glare at me, shake his head, scowl, and spit into the river. I loved it. I understand that my reaction was immature, but I'm still glad that I thought quickly enough to laugh at him and wave again before he turned away.

Ingrid had an experience that summer that proves the natural world (the real world) can always surprise us. We'd discovered a very safe swimming hole in a beautiful location on Canton Creek. The small, deep pool couldn't be seen from the road so was rarely visited by anybody. We liked going there as a family whenever Mike and I could take a couple of hours off together between lunch and dinnertime. On a hot August afternoon, when the cool water was especially inviting, Mike, Pete and I had just climbed out to sit on a streamside rock to dry when Ingrid screamed, "A crawdad's biting me!" Crawdads don't bite, but within seconds Mike and I had pulled her out of the water. We both saw the river otter as it swam downstream through shallow water into another small pool. Ingrid was crying, and the back of her thigh was bleeding from two visible puncture marks. A towel pressed against the wounds soon stopped the bleeding. Back at the inn a guest doctor, a general practitioner, assured us that otters didn't carry rabies. He thought the bites had likely been inflicted by a mother with pups nearby. Ingrid's wounds healed cleanly within a matter of days.

Two days after our summer at the inn ended we flew from San Francisco to Frankfurt. Air travel has changed a lot since then. In 1972 we took a Condor Airlines charter flight. Condor, managed by Lufthansa, charged no more than half that of their parent company. Our plane wasn't full, so we had six seats for the four of us, leaving plenty of room for the children to sleep during the eleven-hour flight. Flight attendants were genuinely friendly and attentive. All the meals were excellent, and good wine was served with dinner, and then cognac after dessert. These days economy passengers are treated something like cattle hauled down a bumpy country road in an overcrowded truck to a feedlot.

Flying is the lowest form of voyaging. One might as well be a lump of shit.

HENRY MILLER (WELL AHEAD OF HIS TIME)

But soon after we reached Bamberg, events at the Summer Olympics in Munich proved how trivial minor discomforts are. Eight members of a Palestinian terrorist group attacked the Olympic Village and took nine Israeli athletes hostage. All the hostages, along with a German policeman, were murdered. My father was devastated over the tragedy. He'd been through a world war, and the deprivations and treatment he'd suffered led to health problems that lasted the rest of his life. Along with most Germans of his generation, he'd hoped that a successful Olympics would improve Germany's reputation in the world.

Something I knew he felt good about was the fact that the two-story home he'd built with his own hands, and where I'd lived nearly all my life until marriage, was big enough to comfortably house my family of four. My brother Herbert, his wife Kaethi and their two children, Robert and Giesala, lived on the bottom floor. We were on the top floor with my parents, with two bedrooms and a bathroom to ourselves.

Our plan was to stay in Bamberg for a full calendar year. Mike, with a desk and typewriter in our bedroom, wrote a book. Soon after we arrived I bought a zither, a difficult instrument with 34 strings, which makes it something like playing four or five guitars at once. I found a music school in town that offered lessons, and practiced every day. Fifty years later, I'm still at it, still making house music as best I can.

An elementary school was in easy walking distance down a hill, just beyond the Catholic Church. Ingrid was enrolled in kindergarten and Pete in fifth grade. My parents were both surprised and pleased about the short time it took them to learn adequate German, local dialect included. As children they had few problems adapting to a new culture.

Pete introduced an American pastime to the boys of Bamberg. He grew up with baseball, and I'd learned about the sport by attending San Francisco Giant games while we lived in the city. The Giants rivalry with the Los Angeles Dodgers reminded me of soccer rivalries in Germany. My father in law knew Joe DiMaggio and got a ball for Pete autographed by both DiMaggio and Willy Mays. He'd given Pete bats, gloves and balls by the time he learned to walk, and we'd brought some baseball equipment with us to Germany. When Mike and I began playing catch with Pete outside my family home on *Hoehenstrasse* the neighbors had no idea what we were doing, or why. *"Es sieht aus wie ein Knoedel,"* the woman next door said in reference to the baseball. (It looks like a potato dumpling.)

We told Pete he might not find any baseball players in Germany, or even anybody who'd heard of the game. But as soon as he was able to communicate with his schoolmates, they began asking him what the strange American sport was all about. Before long their interest had evolved into pick-up games on the fields at the edge of town.

Two or three days a week the doorbell would sound, and then the call: "Pete! Baseball?"

The neighborhood boys' Bavarian baseball games were unique. When there were only three or four players to a side, usually on schooldays, there was only one base. A weekend game might find ten or a dozen boys on a side, and as many as four or even five bases were used to accommodate the crowd. The two gloves we had with us were always used by the catcher and the first baseman. The games came complete with arguments, which always included some name-calling – *Bloedmann, Depp, Esel* (dumbbell, idiot, jackass). Some of Pete's comrades had genuine ability, and they understood the basic rules of the game. The only downside to the Bavarian baseball games came after the two baseballs Pete had brought with him were so worn out that, without telling us, he put the Joe DiMaggio-Willy Mays ball into play, and the autographs were obliterated.

Another American creation – animated cartoons, dubbed in German - were part of our lives that year. German television aired Porky Pig and Bugs Bunny, and also Laurel and Hardy movies. I used the names of the various characters to explain to Pete and Ingrid the extremely literal quality of the German language. In Germany Porky Pig became *Schweinchen Dick* (Fat Pig), Bugs Bunny was *Bunny der Hase* (Bunny the Rabbit), and Laurel and Hardy were *Dick und Doof* (Fat and Dumb).

In the summertime, most often with the children, we hiked along pathways that bordered the river, or that led through the woods or alongside ripening fields of grain dotted with corn flowers and poppies. The point of many of the hikes, as usual, was to visit relatives in neighboring villages.

WATCHING THE
MEN FISH

Through early fall there were powerful thunderstorms, and in winter the weather turned much too cold for baseball - cold enough to freeze the Regnitz River from bank to bank. Mike and I enjoyed Bamberg in any weather – the *Gasthauses*, in particular the Schlenkerla, with its outstanding food and beer. We liked the *Weinstubens* too, offering the local white *Frankenwein*, better than anything we could afford in Oregon.

We went trout fishing just once, in the spring of the year. Herr Asch (Hans), a family acquaintance who owned a factory in Nurnberg, invited us to accompany him and his wife, Luise. We'd visited their large, ultramodern home a few miles outside Bamberg, where Mike made an understandable social blunder. He mistakenly addressed Herr Asch as Herr Arsch (Mr. Ass). Our host turned it into a joke, and to prove there were no hard feelings showed us his wine cellar and gave us a dusty bottle of Italian red to take back to America and save for a special occasion. He used words like *Gerbstoff* (tannic) and *Saeure* (acidity) to describe the wine's flavor. On our way upstairs from the wine cellar he mentioned that he was an amateur artist, and then showed us, in their bedroom, a lovely nude painting of his wife.

Herr Asch was a fly angler, and invited Mike to fish with him on the Wiesent River, not far from Bamberg. It would be a family outing, but only the men would fish. The Wiesent held healthy populations of native brown trout, European graylings, and planted rainbow trout from North America. Fishing access in Germany has little in common with Oregon, beginning with the fact that about 50% of Oregon's land is public, and state residents can hunt and fish on most public lands for moderately priced licenses during designated seasons. For 400,000 Deutsch marks (about $100,000 at the time) Herr Asch had bought the entitlement to fish two-and-a-half kilometers of the Wiesent River near the village of Streitberg. He could fish as often as he liked during designated seasons, or he could sublease the privilege to others. He could also sell his entitlement to someone else whenever he wanted, probably for an even higher price. According to Herr Asch, counts and barons used to hold the rights to German streams, but after the war things had opened up to include the wealthy.

When the day came, a sunny Wednesday morning, Herr Asch picked us up at nine o'clock in a big, shiny, metallic grey BMW. We headed for the Wiesent with the women in the back seat. Like many German men, Herr Asch drove too fast. When we hit the Nurnberg-Berlin autobahn (no speed limits on autobahns) I watched from the back seat as the speedometer needle climbed to 180 kilometers (110 miles per hour). When I politely explained that we weren't used to high-speed driving in America, he slowed down all the way to 160 kilometers, not quite 100 miles per hour.

After slowing down Herr Asch had angled into the relatively slow lane, but moments after that we were passed by a green Mercedes. He muttered something under his breath, swerved back to the fast lane and set out after the Mercedes, but we reached our exit before he could catch up. "*Ich habe gewonnen!*" he said. (I gained on him!)

When we reached the Wiesent Herr Asch wanted to park alongside the road, walk across a meadow, and then across a wooden bridge, where he and Mike would begin fishing. Frau Asch wanted her husband to drive across the bridge and park among the trees alongside the field of rye on the other side. They argued about it. Frau Asch thought the shade across the river looked inviting. Herr Asch argued that shade was shade no matter which side of the river it was on. And he was worried that if he parked across the river, the farmer who owned the land might come and ask him to move the car. Frau Asch doubted that the farmer would show up, and, even if he did, he'd have no reason to bother us. So an angry Herr Asch drove across the bridge to park in the shade of the trees. As he and Mike got their fly rods ready, Frau Asch and I spread a blanket, and then unloaded baskets of food and a cooler of beer from the trunk of the BMW.

A few minutes later the farmer arrived, chugging along the dirt road on our side – and his side – of the river. Herr Asch had to drive back across the bridge. He tried to argue, but it was obvious that the old man on the tractor, bent and weathered from years of labor, enjoyed telling the rich man what to do. We carried the food and beer back to the car, and, face aflame with rage, Herr Asch drove us back across the bridge.

Things soon got worse. No trout were rising anywhere, because no Mayflies were hatching, even though Herr Asch said they should be. He decided to fish with floating Mayfly imitations anyway, because this was the time of year they were supposed to work. Mike didn't say anything, but I watched him tie a small black wet fly – a fly meant to sink - to his leader tippet.

Frau Asch and I sat on the blanket nibbling on bread and cheese and watching the men fish. Herr Asch, downstream from where we were parked, made his way toward us with his dry May fly pattern. Mike, with his wet fly, started far above us and fished downstream, toward Herr Asch.

I saw most of what happened, and Mike filled me in on the details later. The two fishermen were no more than thirty yards apart when Mike hooked a small rainbow trout, quickly hand-lined it in and released it. Then he clipped the fly from his leader tippet and pulled his wallet out of his back pocket. I knew he kept a Skunk steelhead fly in his wallet, the one he'd used when he landed and released his biggest steelhead ever. What I hadn't seen from the car was the big brown trout that had come up off the bottom and made a pass at the little rainbow Mike had hauled in. Now he was hoping that the brown trout might come up again for a fly as large as the Skunk. And it did, on Mike's first cast. He hooked the fish and followed it downstream, the fly rod bowed.

By the time Mike lifted the brown trout out of the water, Herr and Frau Asch and I were there on the riverbank to watch. The fish was gorgeous – at least two feet long, with flashing golden sides and a dark back with dime-sized crimson spots.

"Toten Sie es bitte!" Frau Asch said. *"Wir wollen es zum Abendessen!"* (Please kill it for us! We want it for dinner!")

Mike smacked the trout's head hard against a rock embedded in the riverbank. "It's probably best to kill it," he said. "Best for the river I mean. A big brown like this is a cannibal. It'll eat dozens of young trout every day."

Frau Asch had all the ammunition she needed. With a smile on her face, she told her husband that Mike was a much better caster than he was. She turned to me with her smile to tell me that her husband had never hooked a fish in the Wiesent as big as the one Mike had just caught.

I thought I knew what might be coming. I was right. Twenty minutes later, the brown trout cleaned and stowed with the beer in the cooler, we were traveling down the autobahn toward Bamberg at 180 kilometers per hour.

MORE THERE THAN
I WANT OR NEED

I have a hunger for nonhuman spaces, not out of any distaste for humanity, but out of a need to experience my humanness the more vividly by confronting stretches of the earth that my kind had no part in making.

SCOTT RUSSELL SANDERS

I visited a few old friends who still lived in Bamberg, and I spent a lot of time with my parents. This was before supermarkets established themselves in Germany, and I enjoyed shopping for food with my mother the old fashioned way. Nearly every morning we made stops at a bakery, a butcher shop, and, when the weather was warm, an outdoor fruit and vegetable market. There was lively conversation everywhere we went – a lot of it neighborhood gossip - because the proprietors knew their customers and the customers knew each other.

My sister Elisabeth, her husband Otto and their son Harald lived in an apartment in Nurnberg, and Mike and I visited them often. We went to most of the soccer games that my father refereed on Saturday afternoons. Even in the smallest villages the fans were at the very least enthusiastic, and often enough fanatical. The standard insults that my father heard screamed at him when he made a call against the home team were *Dummkopf* (Dumbbell), *Blinde Kuh* (Blind Cow), *Casper* (Clown), and *Armleuchter* (a useless light fixture on a wall).

We visited relations somewhere nearly every weekend. Wherever we went, coffee and pastries were served formally on Saturday and Sunday afternoons. Pete and Ingrid loved the rich cakes. *Schwarzwalder Kirschtorte* (Black Forest cherry cake) was a favorite, and all four of us worked off the thick chocolate and heavy whipped cream on our long hikes.

I reunited with Elfie, a next-door neighbor who I'd walked to school with through the years. Now she lived in Munich, and we got together whenever she came to Bamberg on short vacations. She was the only person I met all year who played the zither, and she played it well.

On many nights Mike and I listened to AFN (Armed Forces Network) radio while Pete and Ingrid did puzzles, read books or played games. All four of us listened to the AFN American Top Forty broadcast on Saturday mornings. An old friend and classmate of Mike's at Punahou School in Hawaii, Ron Jacobs, produced the show, said to be the most popular radio program in the world. We watched televised soccer with my parents, and everybody in the house – undoubtedly almost everybody in Germany – celebrated when Germany won the 1972 European championship.

Once a week, on Friday nights, Mike and I went with my parents to their combination *Gasthaus*-bowling club, where men drank half-liter mugs of beer and bowled, and wives drank quarter-liter glasses of beer, or glasses of wine, or nothing, and sat and watched their husbands bowl. In European bowling a small wooden ball without holes for the thumb and fingers is rolled down a narrow alley at nine wooden pins. There were only two alleys, and the men took turns using them. Whenever a strike was bowled, everybody watching, whether they wanted to or not, was apparently obliged to scream *Holz* (Wood). Mike bowled as well as the German men, and a few of them resented it. For many women, those were long Friday nights.

Housing a family of four couldn't have been easy for my parents. Sometimes my mother treated me as if I was the same twenty-three-year-old who'd left a decade earlier, not a thirty-three-year-old mother of two. I'd learned to like homemade chili along with Mike and the kids, and when I occasionally cooked it in my mother's kitchen she referred to it as "*das rote Zeug*" – "that red stuff." She was unhappily surprised when Mike stored the two large bricks he substituted for dumbbells for his weightlifting exercises in our bedroom closet. Whenever she knew he was working out, even in mid-winter, she felt it necessary to open all the bedroom windows to air out the room as soon as he was done. And she was upset whenever she heard me speak English to Pete and Ingrid.

Mike's mother came to Bamberg on a Christmas visit. We'd reserved a room for her in a comfortable small hotel, but after one look at it we had to move her to the most expensive place in town, the Bamberger Hof, and that became another matter my mother couldn't understand and didn't appreciate. A more serious issue was the fact that my mother-in-law smoked in the living room. As soon as she left the house, the windows had to be opened wide to a bitter cold.

Through it all, my father did his heartfelt best to keep the peace, and nearly always succeeded. He was a fine man – a *mensch,* some people would say – a person of integrity and honor. He tried to hide it, but showed his disappointment when I told him we'd changed our reservations and were returning to Oregon in July instead of September.

Mike and I had talked it over and agreed. Some of our reasons for the change were simpleminded. For example, when Pete talked about how much he missed hamburgers, I realized, to my own surprise, that I did too. There were no Macdonald's or Burger Kings in Bamberg, so on a sunny spring afternoon we all walked about three miles across town to Warner Barracks, where Mike had been stationed, and ordered burgers at the snack bar. We convinced ourselves they were delicious.

Most of our reasons for an early return made sense. I loved my parents but missed my friends in Oregon. Mike and I both missed easy access to wild country – the country that had made me cry the first time I saw it. We missed camping and fishing on the North Umpqua, long hikes through lovely mountains, the wild, lonely Oregon coast.

I'm now approaching the inevitable end of a long life. I've always loved Bamberg (deservedly a UNESCO World Heritage Site), and I've admired many celebrated

European towns: Paris, Rome, Prague, Vienna, Amsterdam and Brussels among them. I've appreciated American cities too: New York, San Francisco, Los Angeles, Denver, Portland, Seattle. But I've evolved to the point where I think of towns the same way experience has led me to regard computers and i-phones: there's always much more there than I need or want - which reminds me of the fact that when you love wild places, what isn't there is the real reward.

BLUE SKY, WHITE SNOW,
AND OPEN COUNTRY

A world without open country would be a universal jail.

Edward Abbey, *The Fool's Progress*

We'd leased our Ashland house to an American Indian family for a year. Luckily for us, we were offered a place to live until their year ran out. Frank Moore owned 80 forested acres, an old homestead, about five miles downstream from Steamboat Inn. By now he and Jeanne had moved into a log house he'd built high above the river on his property, and he was almost finished with a second house that would become a rental. We stayed in the nearly completed house for weeks, close enough to the North Umpqua to hear the moving water during our quiet nights.

When we moved back to Ashland everything looked to be in fine shape, except for our cat, Herkimer. He'd been overfed and was so fat he looked like a miniature pig with fur. Possibly because he was too slow to hunt and catch anything, the diet we put him on worked. While Herkimer lost weight another animal joined our household – a German shorthair puppy, a pointing dog that we named Otto, after my brother in law. For a few years Mike had been hunting pheasant and quail with a friend who owned a well-trained black Lab. Now that we had our own dog the two of us could hunt together wherever and whenever we wanted.

The months we'd spent in Germany forced me to realize I was an American now, a citizen of the country that, as I saw it, had the most diverse and therefore most interesting population on earth. Many African students enrolled in Mike's classes, and we made friends with some of them. According to Mike, a Nigerian named Johnson Obot was an excellent writer, in English, with a subtle and irresistible sense of humor. Years later he would become a professor of geography in his home country. Stanley, from Kenya, a member of the Masai Tribe, taught me how inaccurate stereotypes can be. When I asked him how close he'd ever been to a lion, he laughed and admitted he'd never seen a lion in his life, not even through binoculars.

Mike's office was a short walk from our house. Pete, in sixth grade, and Ingrid, in first grade, had ten minute walks to reach their schools. With more free time on my hands, I started working part-time at the college, always during registration week, and at other times to fill in for people who were out sick or on vacation. I met new people and made friends. Eventually I turned down the offer of a full-time job because that would have canceled our family's outdoor summers. And even if I'd worked full time, no matter how well I'd done at the job I'd never have earned a promotion without a college degree. A woman who'd been in the financial aid office for years and knew the work better than anyone else didn't have a degree, and, she explained to me, that was why she was never promoted.

My part-time work meant we had more than enough money to do what we wanted, with time left over for volunteering. The pear harvest in southern Oregon happens in late summer and early fall, and Mike and I began teaching English to the migrant workers who appeared at Medford's orchards to pick the ripe fruit. They were men and women ranging in age from their teens to their seventies, and they worked hard, usually in hot weather, their pay based on how many pounds of pears they harvested. Even when they worked themselves to the point of near exhaustion, they gathered after dinner to practice English, and after that to play their guitars and sing. Even now, there must be a few of my former Mexican students out there somewhere, speaking English with a German accent.

Mike and I delivered lunches to elderly shut-ins enrolled in the "Meals on Wheels" program. Many of them were obviously lonely and seemed to care more about having somebody to talk to for a few minutes than they did about the food.

My friend Elfie sent me some sheet music for the zither, and when I thought my playing had improved enough I volunteered to play for residents in nursing homes. During my first informal concert nearly everyone in the room fell asleep. When I apologized to the nurse in charge she assured me that over half the audience members suffered from insomnia, so my music had been a blessing.

Volunteer work was nearly unknown in Germany, and doing it made me glad to be an Ami.

***

Mike built a kennel in our back yard and bought a book on training hunting dogs, and we worked together with Otto. For good results, half an hour of training every day for six months, or better yet a year, is what the book recommended.

We started off with simple obedience training. To begin with, a dog has to understand exactly what the word "no" means. After that it can learn other simple and necessary commands: "stay," "sit," and "come." The ironical command "charge" told Otto to lie down and stay put, wherever he was. The most difficult obedience command is "heel," meaning that, no matter what, the dog has to walk, jog or run close at the left side of the human in charge.

A bird dog needs to learn much more: despite its instincts to range far and wide, it has to stay close in the field so as not to flush birds out of range; to respond to hand signals when making retrieves; to bring dead birds back to hand, even though its instinct is to eat them; to respond to whistle signals – one whistle blast means sit and stay, immediately, and a series of short blasts means come.

By the time Otto was a year old he'd become a well-trained dog, but I wasn't certain I wanted to hunt, or even that I approved of hunting. Should I kill innocent birds? Mike and I talked about it, and I thought about it. I'd always eaten meat, including birds that someone else had killed for me – chickens, turkeys, ducks, geese, and Cornish game hens, whatever they were, all neatly packaged at grocery stores or served in restaurants by polite waitresses or waiters. All Mike intended to hunt were mountain quail, elusive birds that lived in remote country. He wanted to hunt them because almost no one else did, and because hunting them wouldn't reduce their numbers, but would actually increase them. When a dog flushes a covey of a dozen or more quail, they often fly considerable distances in small groups. Some of the groups never reunite with their original coveys, resulting in new coveys created in new places.

During Otto's first fall and winter, Mike and I, without shotguns, hiked the mountains and valleys with him, searching for lonely areas to hunt the following year, when his training would be complete. We reached places so far from roads, and so hard to get to, that we found no evidence to suggest that humans had been there for a long time, if ever – no old campfires or jeep tracks or boot prints or beer cans, no spent shotgun or rifle shells. Normally there was snow in the high country by the end of November, with animal and bird tracks everywhere – deer, elk, bear, rabbits, coyotes, cougars, quail and grouse. On a cold, cloudy morning, walking among Douglas firs, a coyote charged out of a patch of brush a few feet ahead of us and sprinted across a small clearing, disappearing back into the trees. Otto started after the coyote, and when

Mike whistled him back he obeyed. Later that same day we came across a half-devoured deer, a young buck, probably the work of a cougar.

Otto learned to properly use the instincts he was born with: striking scent, trailing scent, and pointing coveys of quail and occasional blue and ruffed grouse holding in heavy cover. A dog on point is beautiful to see - muscles tense, nose twitching, a front leg elevated, still as a statue except for the nose. Mike taught Otto to break point and flush birds with the command "go on," and also taught him not to chase birds after they flushed.

I remember a hike in the Cascades that first year with Otto. November weather had been cold and stormy. Otto struck scent just as we saw quail prints on crusty snow about halfway up a mountainside. Stubby tail wagging in a blur, nose close to the snow, Otto trailed the birds uphill, looking back at us every few seconds, staying close as he'd been trained to do. He stopped short and went on point a few feet from a dense patch of poison oak. We walked up and stopped behind him. When Mike told Otto "go on" he crashed into the brush, the covey flushing with loud, drumming wing-beats in calm, cold air. There were patches of brush interspersed with pines and firs all the way to the top of the mountain, and we watched as the quail, two or three or four at a time, set their wings and settled into cover. We followed them up. When Otto flushed the scattered birds they rose from their cover and, this time, flew downhill over our heads, gaining speed as they went, finally setting their wings to glide on down and out of sight. We stood on the mountaintop with Otto sitting between us. I scratched between his ears. "Good boy," I told him. With the quail gone, all we saw for uncountable miles in any direction was blue sky, white snow, and open country.

I felt my lungs inflate with the onrush of scenery.
SYLVIA PLATH

The next November, during Otto's first hunting season, we began a Thanksgiving tradition that lasted many years. Instead of a traditional turkey dinner our meals featured steelhead and mountain quail, a way we had of giving thanks for what we love. Unless the weather made it impossible, we hunted our quail the Wednesday before the holiday.

Most Thanksgivings our hatchery steelhead came from the North Umpqua. There's no discernible difference in taste between wild and hatchery steelhead. The reason native fish are superior creatures is that they struggled through their young lives to survive while hatchery fish grew up in concrete tanks without a process of natural selection, therefore becoming low-grade adults. Mike wrote a *Sports Illustrated* article explaining why removing man-made fish from the native gene pool was a benefit to both the native fish and their river.

***

After I started hunting mountain quail – trying to hunt them – I doubted I'd ever hit such a fast, elusive bird in flight. When the dog flushes a covey the birds seem to be flying at full speed the instant they leave their cover. Wings drum loudly as they speed off, usually in different directions at difficult angles, often swerving around brush and trees. A straightaway shot is easiest to make, but they don't come often.

I learned how to load the single-shot 20 gauge, how to carry it, and how to cock the hammer with my thumb as I raised the gunstock to my shoulder. I knew I should concentrate on a single bird, start the gun barrel behind it, then swing toward it, and pull the trigger just as the barrel passes the bird, and keep the barrel moving during and after the shot. But the eruption of a covey of mountain quail was so sudden, so thrilling, that I couldn't think calmly and quickly enough to do any of that. I was too slow, too excited, and for a long time I missed every bird I shot at.

***

On the day before a cold, clear Thanksgiving, deep in the Cascade Mountains, we wanted four birds to take home for the holiday dinner. We covered many miles, and by lunch time Otto had found and flushed two sizable coveys from willow thickets close beside a creek bank. Mike killed a quail from each covey and I missed the only shot I took. We sat with our backs against an oak tree and ate smoked hatchery steelhead and dried fruit for lunch, and drank from the creek.

A few miles after lunch, about twenty yards ahead of us, Otto went on a solid point a few feet from a thick patch of buck brush on an otherwise barren patch of land on a mountain slope. "These birds should fly straightaway, uphill," Mike whispered. "I'll stay behind you. Stop a few feet behind Otto. Cock the gun and be ready and then I'll turn him loose. Relax. They should fly straightaway, uphill toward that next clump of brush up there. It's a good forty yards out. Pick a bird and let it get at least halfway there before you shoot."

When I cocked the gun I was close enough to hear nervous birds clucking and scurrying back and forth in the buck brush.

"Go on!" Mike told Otto.

When Otto exploded into the brush birds exploded out, loosely grouped and heading up the hill. The gun at my shoulder, I picked the quail farthest to the right. I had it at the end of the barrel but I didn't rush the shot. It was thirty yards out when I pulled the trigger. There was a puff of feathers and it fell, and then Otto was there to make the retrieve.

"Reload," Mike said. "I think there's more."

I broke the gun open, pulled out the spent shell, stuck it in my pocket, and, my hands shaking, replaced it with a live round and closed the gun. Mike took the dead quail from Otto and motioned toward the buck brush.

"Go on!"

Otto flushed four more quail. I chose the last bird out as it started up the hill, but halfway to the buck brush it made a full turn and came back down, high up and straight over our heads. I had the gun up, the barrel behind the quail, and I swung toward it and slightly past and pulled the trigger without stopping the movement of the gun.

Another puff of feathers, and the quail fell, and Otto retrieved it.

Those were the first two mountain quail I ever shot. I felt neither guilt nor elation. I was content to have proved to myself I could do it.

———————

In intercourse with Nature you are dealing with things at first hand, and you get a rule, a standard, that serves you through life. You are dealing with primal sanities, primal honesties, primal attraction...

JOHN BURROUGHS, *THE GOSPEL OF NATURE*

———————

hunting for mountain quail

VAN GOGH ON OUR
WAY TO MEXICO

The years went by like unmoored boats borne on a river current.

PAUL NIZAN, *ANTOINE BLOYE*

Pete and Ingrid were never seriously troubled adolescents. They did what was expected of them, and required of them, with few complaints. What I remember as a potential serious problem was the fact that by age twelve Ingrid was already a tall, lovely girl. Her height helped her athletically. She became a young basketball star and also set a middle school high jump record in 1981 that still stands. The trouble was that when she walked down our street past the college dorms toward her elementary school, and then back home after school in the afternoon, college boys began approaching her and even asking her out on dates. That was one reason we bought her a horse, an appaloosa she named Eagle. She loved Eagle from the start, and was happy to clean stalls at Linda Davis' Eden Farm and take

English riding lessons from Linda in preparation for competitive three-day events: dressage, stadium jumping, and cross-country. Pete, beginning at age twelve, became an outstanding distance runner who was eventually named to Oregon's all-state high school cross-country team, and then accepted a scholarship to run at Lewis and Clark College in Portland. He inspired Mike, Ingrid and me to add distance running to our list of family recreations.

***

Pete was away at Lewis and Clark, Ingrid was living with friends and working in Honolulu, and Mike was taking fall quarters off because his writing produced enough income to allow it. In November we often drove our old Ford Bronco from Ashland to Loreto, a Baja fishing village 1,500 miles south.

On one Baja trip we were lucky enough to see original Van Goghs. Mike's mother lived within walking distance of the Los Angeles County Museum of Art, and she made reservations for Mike and me to see the extensive exhibit that happened to be in town. His paintings are magnificent, so rich with paint that some of them might not be quite dry yet - and he writes beautifully too, as in a letter to his brother Theo:

> I feel more and more that we must not judge God on the basis of this world; it's a study that didn't come off. What can you do, in a study that has gone wrong, if you are fond of the artist? You do not find much to criticize; you hold your tongue. But you have a right

to ask for something better. This life of ours, so much criticized, and for such good and even exalted reasons – we must not take it for anything but what it is, and go on hoping that in some other life we'll see a better thing than this.

A day after Van Gogh's paintings, the smoggy, traffic-choked early morning drive on the 405 freeway to San Diego was close to depressing. The drive across the border and through Tijuana was worse. Poverty was in plain sight everywhere. We should all be hoping for a better thing than this.

We spent that night 200 miles south of the border, at a hotel in the coastal town of San Quentin. There was no hot water in our room, and hotel employees had a loud party in the room next door that wouldn't end until it was nearly time for breakfast. But that didn't matter much. Toward dark, while we drank wine on our balcony with a view of a long, lonely, lovely curve of beach, we watched flocks of ducks, thousands of them, passing overhead on their southward migration.

The last 500 miles of our drive were mostly through the Sonora Desert. Before I'd ever seen an actual desert I'd expected something bleak, an intimidating desolation. But the sunrises and sunsets – the beginning and end of radiance - are stunning. The clean, wild, silent desert seems to stretch away forever, and it made me feel small, because we are.

Really to see the sun rise or go down every day, so to relate ourselves to a universal fact, would preserve us sane forever.

Henry David Thoreau

We camped just south of Loreto, at Puerto Escondido, described this way in 1940 by John Steinbeck in *The Log from the Sea of Cortez*: "If one wished to design a secret personal bay, one would probably build something very like this little harbor." Protected by mountains on one side and offshore islands on the seaward side, it was an especially ideal bay for small boats, and we had what might have been the smallest fishing boat in Baja - a ten-foot inflatable powered by a six-horsepower Johnson motor. We ended up naming it *Zucarita,* because Zucaritas, a popular cornflake cereal in Mexico, was our morning routine.

We were out on the water with our fly rods before 7 every morning. Mike had a secondhand saltwater fly reel and we'd bought a new one for me in Los Angeles. The streamer flies we used imitated small bait fish instead of bugs. Whenever we saw either surface-feeding fish or birds diving to feed, we got there as fast as our little motor could take us, and from ten or fifteen yards away we cast our streamer flies at the action. But most of the time the calm sea was flat as glass, and then we trolled at slow speed, our streamers twenty to thirty yards behind the boat.

Any ocean anywhere produces surprises. Late on a beautiful morning, about a hundred yards offshore, we saw three men on the beach, one flat on his back on the sand, the other two waving at us. Thinking they were being friendly, we waved back. Then they frantically motioned us to shore and yelled at us through cupped hands. We couldn't hear them over the sound of the motor, but once we reached shore we learned that the man on his back, swimming in shallow water, had been stung by the tentacles of a school of jellyfish known as Portuguese man' o wars. He'd screamed, vomited almost at once, and then passed out. His friends thought he might be dying. We got all three of them into the Zucarita and motored to Escondido as fast as we could go. The ghostly white victim, with ugly red welts across his chest and shoulders, was struggling to breathe. Two Mexican fishermen parked near the dock drove him to Loreto, where, we learned the next day, he was treated and recovered.

On most beautiful mornings all we did was catch bonito, skipjack tuna, sierra, jack crevalle, and cabrilla, and killed one fish of the right size per day, a sierra or cabrilla, for our dinner. What we most hoped for were dorado, called dolphin fish in English and mahi mahi in Hawaiian. The area's most reliable dorado fishing began in July and lasted through October, then tapered off through November. On that first trip we were hoping for a dorado for Thanksgiving dinner, but went days without hooking one, and by the day before Thanksgiving we'd given up hope.

I hooked a big fish late that morning, as we were trolling our way back to Puerto Escondido. After the strike, when Mike killed the motor, the only sound was the nylon backing line hissing off my reel. Whatever it was ran at least 100 yards in a matter of seconds.

"My line's half gone!" I said. "I can't stop it!"

"Let it go!"

Off in the distance I saw the fish jump.

"Dorado!" Mike said. "A big bull!"

It cleared the surface by six feet or more, seemed to hang in the air, came down nose-first, and the rod went dead in my hands. "It's off!" I said. "It's gone!"

"It's coming back at the boat! Reel!"

I reeled as fast as I could, and when the line finally tightened I felt the fish. Then, not far off, the dorado made a series of such quick jumps that it looked as though three or four different fish were out there. After the jumps he circled the boat, forty yards out. I worked him slowly toward us, and then he ran again, and again, and the leader knots and the hook held, and finally I had him close.

"Don't kill him," I said.

"Take a good close look," Mike answered.

With the big hook gripped hard in his right hand, Mike hoisted him halfway out of the water, all gold and blue and green, as beautiful as any living creature could be – and I'd been joined to that power and beauty, that visceral life. When Mike twisted the hook out the dorado dropped into the sea.

"He'll be fine," Mike said.

For our Thanksgiving dinner we cooked ground beef on our camp stove and made tacos, with fresh papaya for dessert.

The dorado wasn't the only luck I had on that trip. On the way home we stopped at Mike's mother's in Los Angeles again and rode a bus to Hollywood Park on a Saturday afternoon for the races. There was a horse named Herr Heinz running, with odds of him winning listed at 75 to one. I bet two dollars on Herr Heinz, and, when he won in a photo finish, I turned in my ticket for $150. Mike wondered whether any horse in racing history had ever won at such long odds. Some people sitting behind us, who knew what had happened, asked me for betting advice for the rest of the afternoon.

A DEEPER, CLEANER BLUE

In late summer most years we canoed along the waterways of Klamath Marsh, when all we could hear was birdsong and our paddle blades moving through water. On the Friday after Thanksgiving, whenever the weather allowed it, we visited the Klamath Wildlife Refuge and Tule Lake. Driving through the refuge, we always saw marsh hawks hunting, and coyotes prowling, and bald eagles perched on cottonwood trees. Tule Lake was a annual stop for flocks of migrating snow geese, and by late November there were usually at least 100,000 of them on the lake, and in an exceptional year two or three times that many. It's the largest concentration of waterfowl in the country, and has to be one of the most impressive wildlife spectacles on earth. The big birds, brilliantly white except for their black wingtips, tend to rise off the water often, and virtually all at once, their wing-beats sounding like loud, enthusiastic applause. Airborne, they separate into long skeins that twist and turn in graceful patterns against the sky.

There are a lot of mountains in Oregon – according to the internet, approximately 3,764. From our dining room window we have a view of the Cascade Siskiyou National Monument, where the Cascade, Siskiyou and Klamath ranges converge. These mountains are within easy driving distance, and a few decades ago there were many years when enough snow had fallen by Thanksgiving for us to start using our cross-country skis.

canoeing at Klamath Marsh

In the beginning we went with friends to Mount Ashland. Pete and Ingrid came along on weekends. On days when fresh powder snow covered a solid base there were hundreds of skiers lined up all day long at the downhill lifts on the mountain's north side. The same snow attracted cross-country skiers to the south side, where there were miles of trails with varying degrees of difficulty. When we skied that side we could see all the way to Mount Shasta, seventy-five miles south.

cross-country skiing in the Cascades

Mt. Ashland was a convenient place to improve our skills, but it was crowded. We began exploring and found nearby areas at lower elevations and easier to reach. We had our chosen mountains to ourselves, and that meant we had to break trail, hard work through a foot of new powder snow, but the effort was worth it.

On clear winter days the sky was a cleaner blue than it ever was in summer. Days when it snowed while we skied were wonderful. Our skis, and birds and animals, made the only tracks across endless expanses of snow. In the back of my mind I was always happy with the knowledge that melting snow in spring and summer fed water to the coastal rivers that sustained the steelhead and salmon we loved.

Back home after a morning of skiing, I liked to play *Leise rieselt der Schnee* ("Softly Falls the Snow") on my zither. It was a winter day when my sister called me from Nurnberg to tell me that my old friend Elfie had been found dead somewhere outside Munich, under the snow. In some manner or other drugs had been involved. It had either been an accident or suicide. Sometimes when I play my zither and think of her I cry.

LOGGING ROADS AND
FOREST TRAILS

Even though Mike and I were both in decent physical shape when we began running, it wasn't easy. Mike started with half a mile on the high school track with Pete, just to see how it felt, and was stiff and sore for days afterwards. I started off jogging short distances with women friends who ran regularly, and the same thing happened to me. But we stuck with it, and enjoyed running the roads in and around town.

On an August evening at my 40th birthday party in our yard, some women friends and I decided to run the Rogue Valley's Pilgrimage Marathon, scheduled for the Saturday after Thanksgiving. All of us were near the midpoints of our lives (assuming we were lucky), and we agreed the time was right. With three months to prepare, we trained together, 50 miles per week, with a 20-mile run every other weekend. I started out with confidence, but after the first 20 mile-run I had misgivings. After the next 20-miler, I knew I could do it. Race day was cold and clear, ideal running weather, and I finished my first marathon in under four hours, which had been my goal. The next morning I woke up suffering more body pain (except for childbirth) than I'd ever experienced – and I was as pleased with myself as I'd ever been about anything I'd ever done. Suffering through something difficult, like childbirth or a marathon, produces intense satisfaction.

During the running boom in the 1980s there were scheduled runs nearly every weekend in southern Oregon, the distances ranging from five kilometers to marathons, and Mike and I signed up for many of them. We ran the Portland Marathon twice, and on our second try, to our surprise, won the husband – wife team competition. Pete and Ingrid ran marathons too, making ours the only family I knew about in which everyone had done that.

Running on paved rural roads was agreeable enough, but once we were in shape to handle hills, the logging roads and forest trails we used were far better. The air was always fresh. We were far enough from civilization to drink safely from creeks. Moving silently through stands of trees, we encountered birds and animals.

Finland is officially the world's happiest country. It is also 75% forest. I believe these facts are related.

MATT HAIG

Earth first! We'll log the other planets later.

REPUBLICAN NATIONAL COMMITTEE PRESS RELEASE

AN UNPOLLUTED NIGHT VIEW
OF THE VISIBLE UNIVERSE

When we ran during visits to Germany my brother and sister in law made fun of us. Living on the ground floor of the family home, they often saw us coming up *Hohenstrasse* after six or eight miles on back-roads through the woods and pathways between fields of grain. Whether they were looking out a window or working in their vegetable garden across the street, we could count on the same question from one or the other of them every time: "*Seid ihr verruckt?*" (Are you crazy?) We were fairly sure that the neighbors who saw us running by in shorts, t-shirts and colorful Nikes, even though they usually smiled and waved as we went by, were thinking the same thing.

Germany in the 1980s was nowhere near as crowded with runners as Oregon, but Mike and I came to know some Bamberg runners we met by chance, and learned about their organized events. We entered a cross-country 20 kilometer run and, on a summer day, were surprised and disappointed when the aid stations offered hot soup instead of water, and then happy to find a true Bavarian beer tent at the finish line.

Back in Oregon, we leased a small octagonal dwelling – we called it a cabin - on Frank Moore's North Umpqua property. We had a living room with a woodstove, a kitchen, a bathroom, and two small bedrooms. Water was piped in from a creek, and a few steps beyond the front door was a quarter-acre pond holding bluegills and bass. Deer and occasional elk drank from the pond in summertime. Wood ducks nested in cavities in trees that surrounded the pond, and robins sometimes nested on our windowsills. Once in a while bats flew from room to room after we were in bed, but when Mike turned a light on they soon attached themselves to a wall somewhere, and he scooped them into a basket, carried them outside and released them into the night.

We used the cabin as a comfortable place to stay during our summer and fall fishing trips. Our only connection to the outside world were two radio stations, one from San Francisco and one from Eugene, that came in after dark. We were too far removed from the North Umpqua Highway to hear traffic, not even log trucks. Before World War Two the east-west narrow dirt road at the top of our gravel driveway had been the only road from Roseburg upriver (the same road where Mildred won her standoff against Loren Grey). Besides fishing, it became a perfect place to hike or run, and temporarily forget about the rest of planet earth. We ended up spending time at the cabin every month of the year. In mid-December we went there, usually with snow on the ground, to harvest our Christmas tree.

My parents visited Oregon only once. We arranged for them to live in a comfortable house owned by faculty friends who were in Norway for the summer. I knew that ever since I'd left Bamberg my father had been wondering what my life in America was like. He was favorably impressed with our modest house on a spacious yard shaded by our tall sequoia tree. A few days after they arrived we had a yard party with many friends, and then spent a few days on the North Umpqua. We took them to Crater Lake and the Oregon coast, and I flew with them to San Francisco for four days to show them around the picturesque city.

I'd become a recreational tennis player, and my parents were amazed with all the opportunities we had without being rich. They saw Mike and Pete play golf on the local nine-hole course, and watched Mike, Pete and I finish a half-marathon in Jacksonville. They saw a Shakespeare play on the festival's outdoor stage without understanding a word of dialogue, but they enjoyed the sword-fights.

Toward the end of their visit my father told me that what made him and my mother happiest was the fact that they'd finally seen that I had a nice house in a pretty town with a good husband and family and many friends. The lucky surprise that ended their visit happened in Oakland, the day before they would board their flight to Frankfurt. A German tourist happened to overhear my parents talking in the hotel lobby, and asked my father if he'd come to California for the game. When my father asked what game he meant, the stranger explained that the Bayern Munich soccer team – almost always Germany's best - was playing in Oakland that night, and tickets were available. For a former soccer player and referee, no trip anywhere could have ended better than that.

***

During one of our November fishing trips to Loreto we met an American couple, the Pattersons, a retired engineer and his wife, who lived there full time in a spacious manufactured home on the beach about half a mile north of town. They also spent time on their yacht, anchored at Puerto Escondido, and they told us they'd like to spend more of their time on the yacht, especially during the hot summer months, but were reluctant to leave their home sitting empty on the beach for extended periods of time. So they offered us their beach home for the month of July whenever we wanted it, and all we had to do was live there and feed their chickens and geese.

Before we'd made our first trip to Baja I'd enrolled in conversational Spanish classes and learned the language well enough to interact comfortably in most situations. Living outside of town instead of at a hotel or campground brought us closer to the Mexican community. We got to know the people who lived nearby, and, because we walked to town and back through neighborhoods at least once every day, and sometimes two or three times, we ended up with many acquaintances and a few actual friends. My favorite Baja neighborhood memory involves an extended family that lived in a crowded home about halfway to town. Walking by one afternoon I happened to have our camera in my purse, and a very old woman, undoubtedly an *abuela* (grandma), was sitting in front of the house on a folding chair between the dirt road and their doorway. I struck up a conversation with her and finally asked if she'd let me take her picture. She seemed embarrassed, and shook her head and tried to refuse, but when I asked again she changed her mind. I took the picture and soon forgot about it, until it was finally developed back in Ashland. The next July, on our first walk to town, I knocked on her door. It must have been a granddaughter who opened the door, and, as I began to explain why I was there, the *abuela* appeared behind the girl. When I handed her the photo an exaggerated cliché became real. Her weathered face lit up. In an instant she looked twenty years younger. She told me that no one had ever taken her picture before. Holding it in both hands, she stared at it, wide-eyed with a beaming smile, for a minute or more. When I told her it was a present for her she looked at me with tears in her eyes, and then went back to staring at the photo. We cried and smiled together.

***

We'd retired the *Zukarita* and upgraded to a 14-foot aluminum boat with a 15 horsepower Mercury motor, so now we could safely reach all the offshore islands near Loreto – Danzante, Coronado and Carmen. The waters near Carmen, fourteen miles out, usually offered the best fishing. On the half-hour run to get there, facing east into a bright red sun rising out of a calm sea, we saw schools of flying fish gliding long distances high over the water on wing-like fins to escape their predators. Bottlenose dolphins often swam alongside us in our bow wake, close enough to touch, while frigate birds turned slow circles high in the sky. Trolling streamer flies along Carmen's eastern shoreline, we hooked and released skipjack tuna, boni-to, cabrilla, sierra, and occasional yellowfin tuna. When we found schools of dorado holding underneath floating lines of Sargasso seaweed, we stopped the boat and cast our streamers to them. Blue and humpback whales some-times surfaced so close to the boat that we could hear their exhalations.

After we'd had enough fishing, usually between ten and eleven in the morning, we beached the boat and walked into warm water with our diving masks. Snorkel-ing opened a new world: fish by the thousands, of every imaginable shape, color and size, swimming with no ap-parent effort over clean white sand and among colossal rock formations. There were sea turtles, and eels and sting-rays that frightened me in the beginning, but I learned soon enough to love them all. Luckily, I never saw a shark.

On the long run in from Carmen Island, sitting in the bow, tired and happy, I enjoyed the cool wind in my face and the view of the steep, rugged Sierra de la Giganta Mountains. On a rare day too windy to fish, Mike and I hiked a steep trail up the same mountain John Steinbeck had climbed with his party before writing *The Log from the Sea of Cortez.* We climbed so high that we were look-ing down on circling turkey vultures.

***

We moored our boat over sand in shallow water in front of our temporary home. Mike would clean the one fish we'd killed, and I cooked it. After *Mittagessen* (midday meal) we took naps, then showered, and, wearing shorts, t-shirts and wide-brimmed straw hats against the sun, we walked to town, sometimes to shop, more often to drink a bottle of beer and talk to people off the fishing boats (*pangas*) that docked behind the stone breakwater.

The conversations were usually about where fish could be found, and sometimes about avoiding trouble. Sooner or later, everyone who fishes often in a small boat faces danger. For Mike and I it happened during a run in from Carmen Island. We were at least three miles from shore when a sudden *chubasco* (squall) hit us. In a matter of minutes a flat sea turned very rough. Wind blew and progressively larger choppy waves slowed us down until we were barely moving. We had life jackets on and wouldn't have drowned, but we might have lost our boat. We were lucky to reach the breakwater, with no more than a few minutes to spare.

A few days after our *chubasco* adventure, the Pattersons invited us to sail with them to Danzante Island, catch some fish for dinner, and spend the night on their yacht in a quiet cove. While they slept below, Mike and I stayed on deck with an unpolluted night view of the visible universe that few people anywhere have ever seen.

WHAT HAWAIIANS CALL
"TALKING STORY"

When Pete was a senior in high school we spent part of Christmas vacation in Honolulu, my first visit to Hawaii. Growing up in Germany we had no television set, and for entertainment I listened to the radio, went to the movies and read magazines, and ended up with naive ideas about both California and Hawaii. In my mind California had perfect weather and girls liked to ride around in convertibles with the tops down and wind in their hair. Nearly everybody was attractive. In Hawaii, well-tanned people spent a lot of time on perfect beaches lined with palm trees, and at night they gathered at luaus where native girls in grass skirts danced the hula.

California hadn't looked much like what I'd come to expect, and neither did Hawaii. In 1955, the year Mike graduated from Punahou School, for the first time in their history the islands attracted more than 100,000 tourists. There were three sizable hotels on Waikiki Beach then – the Moana, the Royal Hawaiian and the Halekulani. By the time I got there the yearly tourist count had passed 10,000,000. Traffic was heavy all day long, Waikiki was mobbed with tourists, and the Moana and Royal Hawaiian, at the heart of Waikiki, were dwarfed by dozens of huge new hotels.

Mike had connections with his Punahou classmates. The school had been founded by Protestant missionary families that reached the islands in the early 19th century, determined to convert the natives to Christianity. One of Mike's friends, who had married into a missionary family, explained the long-term outcome to me this way: "The missionaries came to do good, and they ended up doing well instead."

When the missionaries arrived, the Africans had the land, and the missionaries had the Bible. They taught us how to pray with our eyes closed. When we opened them, they had the land, and we had the Bible.

MARK SEAL, *WILDFLOWER*

On a hot, humid morning, Mike and Pete ran the Honolulu Marathon together, and the article Mike wrote about it financed the trip. We didn't spend much time at our small hotel along the Ala Wai Canal. The man who made the distinction between doing well and doing good arranged guest passes for us at the Outrigger Canoe Club, near the tip of Diamond Head. (Scenes at the exclusive club were included in the 2011 movie "The Descendants.") We spent whole days on the club's private beach, swimming and snorkeling in warm water in December.

On a cloudy day we took an afternoon walk from Waikiki to lower Manoa Valley to visit Punahou School's 76-acre campus. Thanks to a scholarship, Barack Obama attended Punahou, and I remember a scene from his autobiography, *Dreams from my Father*. He visits the campus with a relative who tells him that Punahou doesn't look like a school, it looks like heaven. In 2021-22, the yearly tuition to heaven was $27,716. At that rate we could have enrolled Pete and Ingrid there, from kindergarten through grade 12, for just over $720,000.

Along with the Outrigger Club, we visited the homes of some of Mike's classmates (a few of them descended from missionaries) and whose dwellings felt more like museums than places to live. One of the visits was to Mike's high school girlfriend, and I wouldn't have been very surprised if she'd charged admission to enter her house.

At a Class of '55 dinner in Manoa Valley we were served cocktails by uniformed waiters. A Hawaiian musical group played and sang on a small stage set up in what looked like a library without books. There was no reason to hold anything against the generous family that hosted us – none of us choose our ancestors – but remembering the experience, "The Descendants" comes to mind. To establish a harsh contrast to the lives of the wealthy citizens portrayed in that movie, the opening scene includes traffic jams, sidewalks swarming with glum pedestrians, some of them disabled, and homeless people living in tents.

***

Every June, Punahou School holds class reunions featuring on-campus luaus. The established tradition is that every fifth year, alumni from distant places gather together there. The 25th and 50th reunions (1980 and 2005 for Mike) are given special attention. In 1980 Mike went to his twenty-fifth reunion while I stayed in Ashland for Pete's high school graduation, so my first reunion was in 1985. Ingrid graduated from Ashland High School that year and traveled to Honolulu with us, with plans to find a job and an affordable place to live with three Ashland friends who would soon join her. They all wanted time – wisely we thought - to decide what to do with their futures.

I made my first connections with native Hawaiians on the 1985 trip. One of Mike's closest friends was Curtis Iaukea, a descendant of Hawaiian royalty. He had been a football teammate of Mike's at Punahou, an all-Pac 8 lineman at University of California Berkeley, a professional football player in Canada, and then a professional wrestler. Now retired from wrestling, he ran a concession stand renting out beach chairs and boogie boards on Waikiki Beach near the Moana Hotel. He knew I was uneasy about having an attractive young daughter living so far from home, and he promised he'd look out for Ingrid and help her any way he could, anytime she needed it. He made his offer clear: "Any kind of trouble, I got the connections. Lawyers, beachboys, lifeguards, tough guys. Plenty tough guys. I can whistle and have fifty gorillas here in five minutes."

We went to a party in the back yard at Curtis' house on the outskirts of town. Twenty-five or thirty people were there, including his Australian wife Janette, and the afternoon was filled with talk and laughter – with life. Besides eating sushi and drinking beer, what Hawaiians call "talking story" was the main pastime. I heard stories about surfing, gathering lobsters, spear-fishing, outrigger canoe races, and more.

Besides Janette, Mike and me, the only other *haole* (white person) at the party was an Englishman, Lord James Blears, who had wrestled on the professional circuit with Curtis. Everybody at the party addressed him as Lord, and when I asked Curtis privately about the title he told me the most memorable story of the day. James Blears had been a sailor on a British ship that was torpedoed by a Japanese submarine on March 26, 1944. The Japanese picked up survivors, took them back to their submarine, and began beheading them, one by one. Blears and three other men escaped by jumping into the open sea and swimming away. They were lucky enough to find an abandoned lifeboat, and three days later a U.S. liberty ship found them. The first thing Blears was given to eat after his rescue was a can of peaches. The date was March 29, and every year after that he celebrated his good luck on that date by eating a can of peaches. The English prime minister, and the queen, saw to it that James Blears became a Lord.

At ordinary Punahou reunion gatherings, too many stories featured luxury cars, divorces, expensive vacations, and, above all, money.

***

The Punahou classmate who had married into the missionary set invited us to visit his beach home on Hawaii, so-called the Big Island. When he showed us around the house, on a private expanse of white sand and tall coconut palms, he explained that it sat there empty, and well guarded, for at least eleven months a year.

After two days and nights in the beach house we drove to Kahuku Ranch, where our host, a lawyer, was a trustee. He explained that in 1861 the 184,000 acres we were visiting had been signed over by King Kamehameha IV to a man named Charles Harris for $3,000. The ranch house, made mostly of expensive koa wood, was as big and well furnished as the mansions we'd visited in Honolulu. Still a working ranch, Kahuku had also become a tourist destination for wealthy Japanese men who, for a high price, shot mouflon big-horned sheep. Native to islands in the Mediterranean, the sheep that had been introduced to the ranch were nearly tame, and some of the men who shot them liked to do it up close, with a pistol, while having the act filmed. Our host asked Mike if he wanted to shoot one too and seemed surprised when he turned the offer down.

***

I'd cried when Pete left home to become a student at Lewis and Clark College in Portland. When we left Hawaii for home and Ingrid stayed in Honolulu, I cried again. I also realized that she was doing something like what I'd done to my parents. She took a job as a waitress in a high-end Waikiki hotel where tips were generous. She soon learned to surf, and when Mike and I celebrated my 50th birthday in Hawaii I watched my husband and our daughter surf a wave side by side at Waikiki. Besides work and surfing,

Ingrid trained for the Honolulu Marathon and finished well, took classes at a junior college, and, after working part-time at a pre-school, decided she wanted to become an elementary school teacher. Back in Ashland, she earned her education degree at Southern Oregon U. and has been teaching in town ever since.

THE MAN IN ORANGE
WASN'T FRIENDLY

If people destroy something made by mankind, they are called vandals; if they destroy something irreplaceable made by nature, they are called developers.

JOSEPH WOOD KRUTCH

Mike had been working on a manuscript with an editor named Doug in New York, and the two of them eventually became friends. In September, three months after the Punahou reunion, Doug invited us on a backpacking excursion into northern California's Mill Creek Canyon, between the town of Red Bluff and Mount Lassen, where he owned 2,000 acres of land. He hadn't bought the land as an investment, but to protect it from "development."

In 1911, at age 50, a Yahi Indian had come out of Mill Creek Canyon and appeared at a barn near the town of Oroville. The last living Yahi, he became known as America's "last wild Indian" and ended up at U.C. Berkeley. Given the name Ishi (Man), he was studied by anthropologists while working as a janitor. With no immunity to common diseases, he was often ill and finally died of tuberculosis in 1916.

Doug's land was in the heart of what had been Yahi country, and even late in the 20th century it was very hard to reach. We rented a jeep in Red Bluff and headed east. Soon we were on a dirt road running through ranch land with grazing cattle. Every few miles we came to a locked gate. As a land owner with legal access, Doug had keys to all the locks. Mile by mile, the country got rougher. There were no more cattle, and the only vegetation was small pines and dry brush. Not long after we'd passed through the last gate, we reached what Doug told us was the old Lassen Trail. Nothing I saw looked like a trail. Rocks of all sizes were scattered everywhere, and there were deep crevasses, and endless twists and turns. "Hold on," Doug said with a smile. "It gets worse."

It did get worse, and we finally turned left and started slowly down a sloping canyon wall. I held on with both hands, and after ten or fifteen minutes of bouncing around, Doug braked to a stop. "This is as far as a jeep can make it," he said. "Now we walk. My first trip in here after I bought the land was in a rented car, I think it was a Chevy. I didn't know any better. When I turned the car in afterwards they weren't happy. I told them I'd run over a rock."

We hiked a long way down into the heat of the canyon, through oaks and pines – "digger pines" Doug called them - with Mill Creek glinting in sunlight below us. We were wearing shorts, t-shirts and running shoes, and used our aluminum fly rod cases as walking staffs. I had no trouble with my heavy pack. Mike and I were in marathon shape, and while we'd been at the Punahou reunion Doug had placed sixth in California's Western States 100 Mile Endurance Run.

Doug told us that over a period of many years he'd never encountered a stranger on his land and never found a trace of what we call civilization – not so much as a matchstick, bottle cap or gum wrapper. But there were artifacts left behind by the Yahi people. In the many caves alongside the creek he'd found woven baskets, arrowheads and spear points, grinding bowls, pestles, and, once, a full quiver of arrows. Sheltered on the west side by private ranch land and on the east by roadless wilderness, that's how inaccessible the country was. When Doug had arranged to bring his parents to Mill Creek, they'd traveled in by helicopter.

Up close, the creek was surprisingly large and could have been classified as a river. A tributary of the Sacramento, years back it had supported healthy runs of Chinook salmon and steelhead. But now, by the time it reaches Red Bluff, Mill Creek has been reduced to a trickle, its water drawn off to irrigate crops. The salmon, steelhead and Yahi are long gone.

We camped on a sand beach bordering a large, deep pool, our sleeping bags only a few feet from the water. On our first evening, on my second or third cast to the head of the pool, I hooked and landed a rainbow trout that was big enough for the three of us to share for dinner. After our meal of apples, bagels and trout, we drank white wine we'd chilled in the creek and talked by a campfire. I'd never felt quite so isolated anywhere, and I found it exhilarating. Darkness comes fairly early in September, and the clear night sky blazed with stars. When I climbed out of my sleeping bag sometime early in the morning to urinate, it reminded me of Van Gogh's Starry Night. The next time I woke up there was light in the eastern sky, and I heard a far off coyote howl. Then, fully awake, I felt a strange prickly sensation on my face, neck and arms. I was covered with daddy longlegs, dozens of them, and for two or three seconds I was terrified. It took two or three more seconds to brush them off. They didn't bite, or, even if they did, there was no pain and no aftereffect.

We spent our days fishing the creek and exploring the territory. Every early morning after breakfast – dry granola and creek water flavored with Tang – Doug headed downstream and Mike and I went up. The trout we caught and released in every pool rose to dry flies, muddlers, that served as imitations of the grasshoppers fish often feed on in September.

We discovered large and small stone caves not far above creek-level, and most of them contained artifacts, including stone bowls, remnants of baskets, arrowheads and obsidian chips. The roofs of some of the caves were blackened from cooking-fire smoke. The smallest cave we found was barely bigger than a phone booth, with eight stone bowls lined up neatly on the floor, and we wondered if it might have been a Yahi storage closet. The most spacious cave was the size of a tennis court, its blackened ceiling at least fifteen feet high. Mike and I skinny-dipped in the creek and made love in the cave afterwards.

In the early afternoon of our third day, a short distance upstream from that cave, I was standing in knee-deep water at the tail of a pool, knotting a muddler to my leader tippet.

"Look downstream," Mike said from behind me.

I looked and saw a cloud of white smoke slowly drifting toward us on the mid-morning breeze. Not far behind it was a larger, darker cloud, and behind that came a wall of smoke.

I reeled in my fly line and hooked the muddler to a rod guide. We started off upstream. The canyon wall here was too steep to climb so we had no choice but to stay close to the creek. Within a matter of minutes I could hear the fire. When I looked back I saw a tree burst into flames and then disappear in what looked like an explosion of smoke. As we ran, the smoke grew thicker.

Mike stayed close behind me. When the creek made a turn to the south we came to what we needed, a more gradual slope that allowed us to climb, and we started up, jogging when we could, climbing when we had to, the fire never far behind us. I knew we were in shape, I was sure we'd make it. We couldn't see them, but now we heard airplanes overhead.

"They must be dropping retardant," Mike said. "Are you okay? Maybe we should drop the fly rods."

"No. I mean I'm okay. No need to drop anything."

We climbed a long way with the fire behind us. I lost track of time. Finally we were well above the fire and smoke and could see a plane overhead, shining silver in sunlight. Then, when we reached something close to level ground, there was a parked helicopter, and men dressed in orange running in all directions. When one of them saw us coming he approached us, and we stopped and waited for him. I noticed for the first time that our t-shirts were blotched with red fire retardant.

The man in orange wasn't friendly. "Who the hell are you two?" he asked.

"Who the hell are you?" Mike asked back.

"What the hell you doing out here?"

"Trying to sell fishing tackle to tourists. What the hell are you doing?"

"Fighting fire, that's what. The fire you two maybe started." He looked me up, down, and then back up, with a half smile on his face. "Who are *you*?" he finally asked me.

"Can you help us or not?" Mike asked. "We could use some water if you have it."

"Not," he said. "Can't help you."

"Let's go," Mike said.

"I'm ready," I answered.

We jogged away, up the long hill behind the helicopter, leaving the smoke behind us. It took an hour or more to reach the dirt road that, farther west, connected the ranches. We started west, jogging and walking for more than an hour, a wall of solid smoke north of us, to our right. Finally we saw what looked like it might be a jeep approaching from a long way off. When we could tell for sure it was a jeep we hoped it was Doug. Instead, it was three bearded, middle-aged men, two in front and one in back sitting beside an ice chest. They stopped, surprised to see us.

"Is that red stuff fire retardant?" the driver asked.

"Hell yes it is," the one in back said. "What else could it be?"

"Were you fishing down in the canyon?" the driver asked.

"Sure they were," the one in back said. "Why else would they have fly rods?" He opened the ice chest and handed us two coca colas.

"Thank you," I said.

"You're welcome, ma'am."

We talked to them for a few minutes, the jeep motor running. They were a lot friendlier than the man in orange had been. Heading east to scout out remote deer hunting spots, they'd seen clouds of wildfire smoke rising out of the canyon. The one in back took our empties and handed us two more cokes. The driver shifted gears and told us they'd pick us up in two or three hours on their way back to Red Bluff if they found us still on the road. All three wished us luck.

The cokes helped. After about an hour of walking and jogging, another jeep appeared in the distance, heading our way. We hoped it was Doug, and, when we could see his fly rod propped against the back seat, we knew it was. He seemed as glad to see us as we were to see him, and he had fire retardant on his t-shirt too.

On that narrow road, a cliff on one side and a drop-off on the other, it took Doug a couple of minutes to get the jeep turned around and pointed west. Mike and I climbed in and we started back to Red Bluff. After we told Doug our story, he told us his. At the first sight of smoke he'd known what had to be happening and headed straight uphill for the jeep. On his way he'd run into men dressed in orange. They were prisoners the state sometimes used to fight wildfires. Once he'd reached the jeep he felt sure he'd find us, and he did.

It was dark by the time we reached Red Bluff. The first place we came to that sold food was a Burger King – we saw the obnoxious sign from a long way off – and my hunger made their Whoppers seem delicious. We spent the night at a cheap motel, the first one we came to after the Burger King.

In the morning the fire was under control and most of the smoke was gone. We drove back into Yahi country, parked the jeep, and made our way down into the canyon. The country was devastated, gray ash and charred trees, but our campsite hadn't been touched by fire. We hiked back up to the jeep with our backpacks and sleeping bags, and then drove back to the motel. A representative of California's state government was there to question us. I can't remember what department or bureau he spoke for, or how he found us, but it was clear he thought we'd probably started the fire. He asked us if we'd had guns with us, and we told him no. He asked us if we smoked, and we told him no. Then he asked us if we were *sure* we didn't have guns or smoke, and we told him no again. He checked our IDs, wrote down our names, addresses and phone numbers, and, in the parking lot, wrote down the license plate number of the rented jeep. Then he drove off in a shiny sedan, back toward Interstate 5.

our Mill Creek camp the night before wildfire

TWO WOODEN LEGS, ONE LONG ONE, ONE SHORT ONE

It's difficult, usually impossible, to evaluate our youthful years as we live them. In mid-20th century Germany I nearly always did what I knew I was expected to do, and rarely questioned or thought much about what other people like me did. I wore certain appropriate clothes when I went to certain places. Whether it seemed to make sense or not, I dressed in what was prescribed - like newly polished dress shoes on a hike through the woods on a Sunday afternoon to visit relatives. Our house was always what I'd now call extremely neat and clean. No one ever left anything out of place. Sometimes this neatness obsession resulted in comical experiences during our visits to Germany. Ten years ago, staying with my sister, Mike left his sunglasses on the telephone table just inside the front door, an act that was seen as such a serious violation of protocol that everyone in the family soon heard about it from my sister.

Germany and Hawaii are halfway around the world from each other, and the lifestyles of native Hawaiians I've known are at least half a world removed from the ingrained routines still common to Germans. I remember an afternoon Mike and I spent on Waikiki Beach with three beachboys. Like many beachboys, these had un-conventional nicknames. They were Steamboat Mokua-hi (Mo-ku-a-he), Rabbit Kekai (Kay-kai), and Mike's old friend, Curtis The Bull Iaukea (E-ow-kay-a). Steamboat got his nickname because he'd been born on a steamboat, Rabbit's was based on his reputed active sex life as a young man, and The Bull had been Curtis' bad-guy professional wrestling name.

Curtis called our hotel room one morning to invite us to meet him at his beach concession stand near the Moana Hotel at two that afternoon. Steamboat and Rabbit would be there, as well as some wrestlers who were spending a few days in Hawaii on their way back from Tokyo to the mainland.

It was nearly two o'clock when Mike and I were or-dering lunch at McCully Chop Sui on King Street. "We'll be late getting to Waikiki," I told Mike.

"You don't quite understand the way Hawaiian time works yet."

I started learning about Hawaiian time when we got to Curtis' stand after three o'clock. His wife Janette was there alone running things, so we sat and waited, talking to her. Curtis arrived at about 3:30 with two of his wres-tling buddies, Dusty Rhodes and Tough Tony Bourne. They'd been drinking beer at a Kalakaua Avenue bar pa-tronized by locals.

Janette left for home, and Curtis rented out boogie boards and beach mats to tourists while Mike and I talk-ed to the wrestlers - but the conversation was continual-ly interrupted by Japanese fans who wanted autographs and photos of their heroes. When Steamboat and Rabbit finally joined us sometime after four o'clock, the wrestlers headed back to their nearby hotel.

Neither Steamboat nor Rabbit said a word about being more than two hours late, or possibly didn't realize they were late, and so weren't. Curtis put up his "closed" sign, in both English and Japanese. The most obvious truth about Curtis The Bull, Steamboat and Rabbit was that they were happy men. No one mentioned politics or money that day, or had anything bad to say about anybody who wasn't there. They talked story, mostly about the old days, sometimes about random harmless gossip they'd heard on what Hawaiians call the "coconut wireless."

Steamboat told about a secret place he knew across the island at Laie Beach, where he could fill a gunny sack with lobsters in half an hour. He was proud of his son, a football player at Brigham Young University in Utah. Rabbit talked about teaching tourists from the Royal Hawaiian Hotel to surf, including two *ui* (beautiful) young movie actresses. What he couldn't understand was why so many people made a fuss about movie stars, because they weren't anything but people. Curtis talked, and laughed, about his San Francisco wrestling match against Haystack Calhoun. At 600 pounds, Haystack had flattened him. "It's all in the script," Curtis said with a laugh. Then he told about a match early in his career, in Klamath Falls, Oregon, where he'd faced an opponent who came into the ring wearing a cowboy hat and carrying a lariat. Curtis made short work of the cowboy and ended up tying him to a ring post with the lariat. The local Modoc Indians in the crowd, who cheered the result wildly, waited for Curtis outside the gymnasium and took him out on the town. "It wasn't much of a town," Curtis said. "But those Indians loved me. I guess they didn't know it's all in the script!"

Steamboat laughed and shook his head when he told Mike and me about his old friend Chick, who had been head beachboy at the Royal Hawaiian Hotel for decades. On the coconut wireless Steamboat had heard that, now retired, Chick was thinking of selling at least some of his treasures. "Every night before he went home, around now, around this time, Chick combed the shallow water an' the beach in front the Royal. Kept what he found in a big sack in his shed. He picked up plenty money. Spent most of it too. Those Japanese tourists like packing their cash around an' it plenty times washes out when they swim. Chick found diamonds sometimes. Bracelets, rings, necklaces, all kinds jewelry. Watches too, but saltwater makes the watches *mea ole*. Broken that means. Plenty false teeth he found. A wooden leg. No! *Two* wooden legs! One long one, one short one! Plenty bathing suits. Men bathing suits, no *wahines*. But how'd those men get back in the hotel an' then on a elevator bare-ass? That's what I want to know!"

The sun dropped into the sea behind streaks of orange clouds at the horizon. Nearly all the tourists were gone from the beach, and most surfers had paddled to shore. Two local boys who worked for Curtis loaded up his van with beach chairs and boogie boards and then sat in the van waiting for their boss. We stayed where we were until well past dark. I liked watching the shore-break waves with the hotel lights reflecting off the water. The beach-boys talked about how the ocean had sustained Hawaiians for thousands of years. Fish, lobsters, shellfish, seaweed, taro roots to make the poi, more than anyone could ever need was there for them. Hawaiians were the first surfers. Riding waves was almost a religion. Maybe it was a religion. But missionaries tried to outlaw surfing. After the missionaries came Hawaiians lost nearly everything, but nobody could take away the ocean. Nobody could kill the waves. Rabbit told about the time Duke Kahanamoku had ridden a first-break wave from way out near Diamond Head all the way to the beach where we were talking story. Duke had won five Olympic swimming medals, three of them gold.

"That long ride on the Waikiki wave was as important as those medals," Rabbit said. "*More* important! Duke brought surfing back. All us beachboys love it on the beach here. That's why we're here. Duke loved it too."

Even if you never have the chance to see or touch the ocean, the ocean touches you with every breath you take, every drop of water you drink, every bite you consume. Everyone, everywhere is utterly dependent upon the existence of the sea.

SYLVIA EARLE

"We had to make sins out of what they thought were natural actions," said the missionary.

SOMERSET MAUGHAM

Years later, my grandson Billy would tell me about people in other places with their own distinctive ways of looking at life and living it. During the summer he spent in Spain teaching basketball to boys at a summer camp, three camp employees he got to know invited him to a party on a weekend night. They said they'd pick him up at ten o'clock, which seemed like a late start for a party. At eleven o'clock no one had showed up, so Billy thought they'd forgotten about him and went to bed. But his friends arrived at midnight and drove him to the party, which didn't end until dawn. They had their own version of Hawaiian time in Spain.

FROM ROME, ITALY, TO
ROSEBURG, OREGON

Life on Earth is at the ever-increasing risk of being wiped out by a disaster...

Steven Hawking

Mike was stationed in Bamberg when the Berlin wall went up, and almost thirty years later, soon after it came down, we traveled to Bamberg. As usual, our flight landed in Frankfurt. But this time, the moment the wheels touched down the plane veered sharply to the right, obviously out of control, with luggage flying from the overhead compartments. At a high rate of speed we crossed runways, barely missing parked planes. Everyone onboard had to be terrified. The amazing thing – it struck me even then, as it happened – was that there were no screams, no outcries of any kind. Passengers sat silently, seat belts buckled, as we skidded across a busy airport. My guess is it lasted no more than five or ten seconds, and soon after we came to a stop the plane was surrounded by fire trucks and ambulances. Some passengers suffered minor cuts and bruises, nothing that needed serious medical attention. Busses arrived to carry us safely to the terminal. Before dark that evening, Mike and I were in old town Bamberg drinking smoked beer at the Schlenkerla. At the table next to ours, fellow customers were talking about the near-disaster that afternoon at the Frankfurt airport.

***

On that trip we made two visits I remember well. My brother had come to know a family in the town of Saalfeld, in the former East Germany, and we drove there to spend a day with them. It was a less than two-hour drive, and reminded me of the fact that if the American army had been a little slower, or the Russian army a little faster, I'd have ended up in East Germany myself.

The Schneiders, mother and father with two daughters, told us stories about how awful, even frightening, life had been under the Soviets. Sandra, the oldest daughter at sixteen, spoke six languages, including the fluent English that she practiced with Mike and me. She showed us comic books that had been handed out to the students at her school with Americans and West Germans depicted as either sadists or homicidal maniacs, or both. As a twelve-year-old, after Sandra had shown promise as a competitive swimmer, a sporting functionary representing the government delivered pills to her at home, never explaining what they were, but ordered her to take them as outlined on a printed schedule he gave her. Her parents threw them away and, when questioned, Sandra claimed she'd taken them. Eventually she was dropped from the East German athletic curriculum.

The Schneiders' small house was clean and neat, their large vegetable garden was flourishing, and the family exuded contentment. A week after our visit to Saalfeld we drove with my sister and her husband Otto to Prague, about four hours from Bamberg. In villages we passed through storks were nesting on many chimney tops, which was believed to bring good luck.

In Prague, for the first and only time in my life, I saw an entire city full of cheerful residents. Arriving in town, pedestrians we drove by smiled and waved at the car. When we parked and got out to walk to a nearby hotel, strangers on the sidewalk who looked at our German license plates smiled and said "Guten Tag." Our two comfortable hotel rooms cost about twelve dollars. Once we'd checked in we asked directions and stopped for beers and dinner at a pub near the Old Town Square, and the bill for four came to less than ten dollars. During our two days and nights in Prague we walked for miles through the city, including three or four trips back and forth across the famous Charles Bridge (construction began in 1357 under King Charles IV), and I never saw a sign of negativity anywhere.

Having been set free, these people were understandably happy, and seeing them that way made me happy. But I knew that reality would set in soon enough. Cities can be wonderful, sometimes exciting, but not for everybody, and not often for very long. From Rome, Italy to Roseburg, Oregon I've observed people living their lives.

Anywhere in this world where large numbers of humans find themselves in close quarters for prolonged periods of time, decadent human behavior has to be expected. The natural world, the unspoiled outdoors, will almost always be a better place. Mark Twain makes this theme clear in *Huckleberry Finn*. Whenever Huck and Jim find themselves alone on the Mississippi River, catching catfish, listening to birds, speculating about the nighttime stars, they're happy. Whenever they're in a town and have to deal with people, something more or less awful happens. Twain could have titled his novel *Nature Is Good, People Are Bad*. That would have been both an oversimplification and an exaggeration, but often enough that's how the world is.

The city, regardless which one it is, does provide a certain degree of sophistication and intellectualism. It offers the challenge of professional matters. It throws new and interesting people in one's path. There is a dynamic and energy in cities which is diametric to life-forces of the forest. Still the cabin is the wellspring, the source, the hub of my existence. It gives me tranquility, a closeness of nature and wildlife, good health and fitness, a sense of security, the opportunity for resourcefulness, reflections and creative thinking.

ANNE LABASTILLE

I ALWAYS TOUCHED THE CINNAMON-COLORED BARK

I have sometimes been wildly, despairingly, acutely miserable, racked with sorrow, but through it all I still know quite certainly that just to be alive is a grand thing.

AGATHA CHRISTIE

Well into middle-age, I was as happy as I'd ever been. Our children had become responsible adults with lives of their own, and Mike and I were healthy with more than enough free time to enjoy our much-loved outdoor pastimes – fly-fishing, upland hunting, cross-country skiing, running forest trails, and, as a recent addition to our list, we'd added mountain biking. Living sensibly, we had money enough to travel to places we loved and wanted to return to – Baja, Hawaii and, of course, Germany.

Then, self-examining on a summer morning, I felt a small lump in my right breast. After a mammogram our doctor diagnosed it as cancer. Mike was with me in his office when he told me, and I cried. My first thought was that old age had arrived ahead of time and might not last much longer. The day after the diagnosis, when I told Pete and Ingrid I had cancer, all of us cried. I wondered if I'd ever see my children married, ever see my grandchildren. I'd always watched my diet and exercised, and I knew I was – or should have been – as healthy as any woman my age that I knew.

I tried not to feel sorry for myself. There were important choices I had to make, and I finally decided on a lumpectomy, the removal of the tumor and surrounding tissue, instead of a mastectomy, removal of the breast. My surgeon, an unfriendly middle-aged man, had an excellent professional reputation, and lived up to it. The operation went well. Lymph nodes were removed and diagnosed, and the cancer hadn't spread. All the doctors and nurses involved in my treatment were efficient and kind. Sometimes I thought they were too friendly, out of pity, and that made me feel worse. Three days after surgery I was home, and three weeks after that I began my radiation therapy – five days a week for five weeks, with weekends off.

At first I felt that the hospital was a sterile environment. Or "institutional" might be a more accurate word. Whatever it was, my appointments were in mid-morning, and to prepare myself for them I went on early morning hikes with Mike on the Toothpick Trail in the Rogue River National Forest above Ashland. We walked a few miles out and back among mostly Douglas firs and madrones, and often saw deer, grouse, pileated woodpeckers, and the usual hawks and turkey vultures circling above the trees.

The biggest tree on Toothpick Trail was a giant ponderosa pine. It grew alongside the trail, and every time I walked by it the same thought struck me – the ponderosa had been here for a long time, and would still be here long after I was gone. Out and back, I always touched the cinnamon-colored bark with my fingertips.

External beam radiation was administered while I lay on my back, perfectly still, confined in a white tube, for fifteen minutes that seemed longer. With my eyes closed I saw the Toothpick Trail, the birds and animals, and my hand felt the rough bark of the ponderosa.

The hikes, along with weekends on the North Umpqua, saved me. For five weeks we drove to our cabin on Friday evening and stayed until Sunday afternoon. For entertainment we had wood ducks with their ducklings on the pond outside our door, and a robin nest with four blue eggs in it on our bedroom windowsill. Nearly every day an osprey circled the pond looking for bluegills, while Steller's jays scolded from the fir trees beyond the pond. Occasional deer wandered by to drink. After five straight days at the hospital this was the perfect place to be.

Because it wasn't crowded even in summertime, we usually fished the upper river a few miles above Steamboat Creek. We were out of bed by 4:15 a.m. for coffee, orange juice and bowls of instant oatmeal, and then on the river from 5 a.m. until 9, when we drove downstream and stopped at the inn for a real breakfast. A lot of people there knew us and some of them asked why we were fishing on crowded weekends. When I told them why, they reacted first with surprise, and then with sympathy and good luck wishes I could tell were sincere. Back at the cabin we showered, then sat outside with coffee and read books with conversation breaks to talk about what we were reading. After mid-afternoon naps we ate early dinners and were back on the water from 5.p.m. until dark. All that exercise tired me out, but at the same time I could feel my strength returning.

A memory stands out. Because of steep, rocky banks, many of the upper river pools are considered challenging even for healthy young men. The road there runs far above the river, and sometimes I wondered whether I was too old, or too sick, to make it safely down to the water and back. My favorite pool called for an especially demanding climb. It had been named Spot X by our friend Dan Callaghan. The name was meant to indicate that the pool would remain a secret kept among friends.

I accepted the challenging climb our second Sunday morning on the river. On our way upstream we fished two other often productive pools, Swiss Cheese and Panther Leap, without raising a steelhead. We arrived at Spot X with the river in shade and sunlight on the mountaintop across the road. Seen from above, the Spot X pool was long and deep, with an enormous gray boulder at midstream, its rounded top far above the surface. Upstream from the boulder the river was deep, with a slow, steady current, and downstream a wide gravel-bottomed riffle narrowed to become a powerful chute of whitewater. Steelhead most often held at midstream, just above the boulder.

My wading staff in one hand and my fly rod in the other, I followed Mike down the steep bank. The jagged rocks of all shapes and sizes we had to navigate were results of the dynamiting that had made way for a paved road.

I made it down safely.

"I might not hook one," I said. "But it doesn't matter. It's wonderful to be here."

We walked across rocks as rounded as cobblestones toward the water's edge.

"What fly do you have on?" Mike asked me.

"A green-butt skunk."

"That should do it."

I waded out through waist-deep water to the rock I always stood on to fish Spot X, about twenty yards above the midstream boulder. Mike stood on the bank behind me and off to my left, so as not to interfere with my back-cast.

Practicing fly-casting in our back yard was always enjoyable. It's a skill that looks easy until you try it and realize the kind of timing and coordination it requires. In a river it's beyond enjoyable, because you're in a river, with its sights and smells and sounds, the timeless current moving against you, just as it's moved for hundreds of thousands of years. I stripped ten or twelve feet of fly line off the reel, letting the current carry it downstream. When the line straightened the green-butt skunk sank, and I pulled off another yard of line, lifted it off the water and made my first cast, quartered downstream. The idea is to keep the line as straight as possible while the fly, just under the surface, slowly swings across the holding water. The hard part is mending the line gently enough so as not to move the fly.

One reason I liked Spot X was that if I made a straight cast, little mending was necessary. There were no cross-currents or eddies, just a smooth, slow flow over the gravel bottom all the way to where the fish held in front of the boulder, about sixty feet from where I stood. My first short cast was good. Now I'd strip another yard of line off the reel after each cast.

A competent steelhead angler who knows a river well is happy to average one hooked fish per day. Just as my line reached the end of its very first drift of the day, a steelhead hit the green-butt Skunk hard and was into its downstream run before I understood what had happened, before I believed it. I was shocked and dazed. Fifty yards below the boulder the fish jumped high, crashed back down and ran again, all the way to the tail of the pool, where it finally stopped and held.

"I saw it come up for the fly," Mike said. "I never heard of anybody hooking a fish where that one came from."

"It looked big when it jumped."

"It came up really fast. It wanted that Skunk. Way to go."

Mike waded out to help me off my rock, and I followed my fish down, reeling all the way to keep the line tight, stumbling over the cobblestones.

The long downstream run had tired the steelhead. Once we reached the tail of the pool it took no more than five minutes to work it into shallow water.

"How big?" I asked Mike.

"At least ten!"

My Spot X steelhead, with a clipped adipose fin, was a hatchery female. To do the river and its native fish a favor I knew I should kill it, but I felt I had to give this female another chance.

Those who contemplate the beauty of the earth find reserves of strength that will endure as long as life lasts. There is something infinitely healing in the repeated refrains of nature – the assurance that dawn comes after night, and spring after winter.

RACHEL CARSON

YOU'RE DAMN SURE ALL RIGHT
IN MY BOOK, MA'AM

For more than thirty years we'd lived in our comfortable house within easy walking distance of the university, and we'd never given a thought to living anywhere else. But after Mike retired from teaching to concentrate on writing, and I retired from office work along with him, we got an unexpected opportunity. Ingrid and her husband Ron and two sons, Billy and Jake, lived in a log house a few miles out of town, and their elderly next door neighbors decided to move to California to be closer to their children. They asked us if we'd be interested in buying their house. They didn't want to deal with realtors, and we made an offer and bought it. Our son Pete and his wife Susan, with their daughter Dana, moved into our town house.

Outside the city limits we'd be living on an acre of land with a septic tank, a well, and what was known to be a fairly unreliable irrigation system. We bought the hoses and tools we needed, a weed-eater, and a chainsaw. The Schrader wood stove in our new living room came as a blessing. We'd learned from campfires and the North Umpqua cabin that nature provides more restful warmth than heat pumps.

Ours was the smallest lot in the area, with most of our neighbors occupying anywhere from three to five acres, and a few of them operating small farms and ranches (and recently marijuana grows) on more land than that. Besides Ingrid and her family, the only person we knew in the vicinity lived down a long hill from us, and across two-lane highway 66. Linda Davis had taught Ingrid English riding and now owns and runs a nonprofit 22-acre horse sanctuary that houses and cares for neglected and abused animals.

What surprised me most after our move were the many near and distant neighbors we soon met, usually when we were out walking, running, or riding our mountain bikes. People working in their yards or fields, and driving pick-up trucks or tractors, waved and smiled, and started conversations. Books and movies had suggested to me something of what the old American west had presumably been like when life was often hard and citizens were expected, even required, to help one another out when help was necessary. Even though we'd lived in the house in town for three decades, we knew few people on our own block. Now, a few miles out of town, we came to know dozens of people. They helped us deal with irrigation, plumbing problems, testing well water, pruning fruit trees, trapping rats, dealing with raccoons. They invited us to their homes for dinner, and we invited them to ours. Most of them had more money than we did, and were far to our right when it came to politics, but that didn't matter much. Decent traces of 19th century America had apparently survived.

On an early morning not long after we'd moved into our house on Reiten Drive, Mike and I were walking east on Reiten toward Emigrant Lake when a rancher we'd seen before but hadn't yet met was coming down the road toward us on his tractor, carrying bales of alfalfa hay to cattle that grazed in a pasture we'd already passed by. I was surprised when he waved at us and pulled over, then motioned us to cross the road to where he'd stopped.

He half-smiled, politely said good morning, and gave us a warning. "Thought you new neighbors out this way oughta know. Some folks on down the road had a break-in two nights ago. I heard about another one three, four weeks ago on that spread up toward the top of Neil Creek Road."

"Thanks for telling us," Mike said. "I guess maybe I should load our shotguns."

When there's no ethical harm to be done, my husband believes in talking to people in whatever vernacular they'll likely feel comfortable with. But I was surprised at what came out of my mouth, without a conscious thought: "Anybody who messes with our place will be toast."

At that the rancher really smiled, and extended his hand. "You're damn sure all right in my book, ma'am! I want to shake your hand!" And he did.

Two or three days after I'd earned a stranger's handshake by making myself sound like a trigger-happy nitwit, I took a leash and collar and offered to take our closest neighbor's dog for a walk. I'd never seen the animal out of its fenced front yard and thought it might enjoy an hour of new sights, sounds and smells. But I was used to well-trained bird dogs, and soon learned that our neighbors – like an apparent majority of Americans - weren't familiar with dog training. This was a fairly large animal, and every time it saw a squirrel, or a low-flying bird, or a covey of quail, no matter what I yelled – *"No!" "Stay!"* – it dragged me toward whatever it wanted to chase. It also jumped up on me more than once, undoubtedly trying to be friendly, but the claws on a front paw drew blood on my forearm. I stayed on friendly terms with our neighbors but never volunteered to walk anybody's dog again.

Later that month I invited the members of my book club to meet and spend the weekend at our North Umpqua cabin. They were women I liked very much, and we enjoyed ourselves. The book I'd chosen for that month was *Into the Wild* by John Krakauer, and after a lively discussion we hiked the south bank river trail from Wright Creek to Steamboat Inn for lunch, and then drove downstream to a wildflower show in the small town of Glide. That night we drank wine and talked more about *Into the Wild* around a campfire between the cabin and the pond. I knew I probably shouldn't play the joke that came to mind, but I'd probably had a little too much wine and did it anyway - I excused myself, walked into the cabin, got my old single-shot 20 gauge shotgun out of a bedroom closet, and carried it back outside. Walking toward the campfire, I held the gun up in one hand. "It's not Alaska," I said, "but it's lonely out here in the Oregon woods. Don't worry though, we'll be safe."

I was certain none of these women had ever touched a gun, and I couldn't miss the stunned looks.

"Is that thing loaded?"somebody asked.

"It's not, but I know where the shells are."

No, I didn't have a lot in common with these people. They had grown up in America, and I hadn't. They had degrees, and I didn't. None of them had ever gone hunting or fly-fishing, or cross-country skiing or mountain biking. But that didn't mean we couldn't be friends.

Guns, she was reminded then, were not for girls. They were for boys. They were invented by boys who had never gotten over their disappointment that accompanying their own orgasm there wasn't a big boom sound.

LORRIE MOORE, *LIKE LIFE*

Later that year I visited my widowed sister Elisabeth in Nurnberg. Her favorite pastimes were shopping for clothes, eating out, and playing gin rummy. She was overweight and didn't believe in any form of exercise. Whenever I invited her take a walk with me, she told me she didn't like to walk. When I suggested we climb the three flights of stairs to her apartment for a little exercise, she explained that use of the elevator went with the rent she paid.

Not long before I'd arrived, she'd spent five thousand Euros on facial plastic surgery that, as far as I could tell, produced no visible results. Two years before my visit, her husband Otto had shot himself in the head after the company he worked for discovered he'd embezzled a large sum of money. Since then she'd become estranged from Harald, their only child. She was helpful, friendly, and always generous. Mike joked that the Christmas package she sent us every December contained at least fifty thousand calories. Like everyone else on the German side of my family, Elisabeth had never known or cared much about what's generally called "nature." But Elisabeth and I still enjoy frequent long talks over the phone, and, every December, despite what I've tried to explain to her, she still sends a large package containing a variety of sweets. Our favorites are the *Lebkuchen* gingerbread cookies, a Nurnberg specialty.

I love her.

DRINKING CUPS OF HOT COFFEE
AND TALKING TO A GOAT

Living two blocks from a university, we'd been no more than a short drive, or better yet a hike or a run, from unlogged forests, healthy streams, wild birds and animals. From our living room window we had a view across the valley to Grizzly Mountain, and our back yard gave us quiet privacy.

After our move out of town we convinced ourselves that we didn't merely live close to nature, we were actually living in it. I counted forty-five mature trees on our property – Douglas firs, Jeffrey pines, incense cedars, white and black oaks, and, planted by the previous owners, spruce, apple, cherry and pear trees. From our dining room window we can see for many miles in three directions. Straight ahead, due east, is the heart of the Cascade-Siskiyou National Monument, an area that's been labeled "an ecological wonderland." The sunrises, on clear and partly cloudy days, at any time of year, are elegant, and so are the rainstorms and heavy snows that teach us not to take the pleasant days for granted. Once a month, not long after dark, a full moon ascends into the black sky over Soda Mountain.

Sitting at breakfast, flocks of Canada geese often pass overhead, sometimes directly above the house, moving from a night on Emigrant Lake to the pastures, and the golf course, where they feed. Between flights of geese we watch, from a few feet away through the glass door to our deck, the birds that come to feed on the seeds we put out early every morning.

In springtime and early summer, while Mike and I drink coffee out on the deck after our morning walk, we watch the courtship flights of red-tailed hawks. Like many bird species, Canada geese included, hawks mate for life. The turkey vultures that arrive from the south in March turn slower, wider circles than the hawks. Both bald and golden eagles sail in from the east to perch at the top of our tallest Douglas fir. Now and then flocks of wild turkeys feed on insects close to the house, where the grass is mowed.

Raccoons roam around at night, so we can't leave suet in a bird feeder. During the darkest nights, owls often hoot from the back yard cedar tree. A coyote killed one of our two cats. We've seen bobcats and foxes walk by in midday, acting as if they'd been domesticated. Deer are common, and during dry summers, desperate for water, they empty the birdbath three or four times a day. Early one summer a doe nursed her two fawns just outside our bedroom window nearly every morning for a month.

Down a hill and across highway 66 we have a clear view of one of Linda Davis' pastures, where six of her rescued horses are turned out from their barn stalls early every morning. They crowd through a narrow gate and gallop across the tree-lined pasture, beautiful, powerful animals, healthy and free. Every time I see them I remember Ingrid riding Eagle in three-day events, and how I closed my eyes whenever they made a jump on a cross-country course.

Besides Linda's horses, other domestic animals, near and not so near, surround us: pigs, chickens, geese, black-belly sheep, dairy cows, steers, llamas - and goats. One winter morning when Mike went out for the paper, a half-grown brown and white she-goat was standing in the middle of Reiten Drive, not a safe place for an animal. A small herd of goats inhabited a roofed shelter in the middle of a fenced field not far beyond our mail box, and this one must have somehow escaped. Mike tried unsuccessfully to urge it down the dirt road across from our driveway, toward its apparent home, but the animal refused to go in that direction. Instead, it ended up following Mike down our driveway to the house. We had no idea who owned the goats in the field across the road, and I couldn't find a listed phone number for either of the two families that lived closest to the fenced field and shelter.

She turned out to be very friendly. After I joined Mike in the backyard she followed close behind us everywhere we went. Finally Mike opened the garage door and she followed me in, but when I hurried back out and we closed the door she became agitated, bleating constantly. So we opened the door, led her out to the back yard, and then up onto the deck. For a while she ate bird seed from a bowl near a statuette of Saint Francis while we watched from the dining room. When she saw us she began to butt the window, hard enough so that we thought it might shatter the heavy glass. We saw no choice but to go back outside and keep her company. She wore a collar, so Mike finally hooked a dog leash to it and thought he'd walk her back down our driveway, across Reiten Drive, and down the dirt road, but she refused to go in that direction. Her clear preference was spending time with us on the deck, so we ended up there, drinking cups of hot coffee and talking to a goat on a cold winter morning.

It was Friday, garbage collection day, and finally I heard one of the neighbors from across Reiten coming up the dirt road in his tractor to drop off his garbage cans. The goat didn't belong to him, but he promised to alert the owner, and half an hour later a teenage boy arrived, thanked us sincerely, gathered the animal up in his arms and carried her away.

Things like that don't happen in town. The longer I live in the country, the more I love it.

How you live your life is up to you. You have to go out and grab the world by the horns. Rope it before it ties you down and decides for you.

Sarah Reijonen

STILL FEEDING WOOD
TO THE FIRE

Many unrelated adjectives can be applied to the ways Honolulu and Waikiki Beach have been "developed" since Mike left the islands for college in 1955 – phenomenal; profitable; alarming; unbelievable; depressing; repulsive. No matter what word you choose, Hawaii has changed more in less than three-quarters of a century than my hometown has in more than 1,000 years. In Bamberg, ancient buildings are preserved, not torn down to make room for something modern and more commercial.

But as time passes people change everywhere, and Germans have been modernized along with the people of Hawaii. Families rarely take long weekend walks to villages for *Mittagessen* (midday meal) and then long walks back, burning off calories. Nearly everyone who's old enough to drive a car has one, so they drive. When I sit in a Bamberg café in the 21st century with a cup of coffee and some *Zwetschgenkuchen* (prune cake), I watch people, especially the young, and they don't flirt the way we did in my day. Instead, as in America, even when they're in groups they spend most of their time staring at their phones. I can visualize a *Fraulein* (young woman) strolling down the sidewalk with her *Freund* (boyfriend), both staring intently at their phones, and when the *Fraulein* disappears down an open manhole, the *Freund* doesn't notice and never loses a step.

You go back home and everything you wished was the same is different and everything you wished was different is still the same.

CORMAC MCCARTHY, *CITIES OF THE PLAIN*

A schoolmate and old friend of mine sent her son Walter to Ashland to spend a summer month with us in Oregon. Walter was the same age as Pete, and the month went well despite a lengthy heat wave that, day after day, produced temperatures above 100 degrees. Within days after his arrival, Walter and Pete competed in a local all-comers track meet despite the heat. After the meet, Ingrid told us that some of her friends were in love with Walter. When Walter learned of a rodeo in a small Northern California town, he peddled all the way there and back, close to 100 miles of mountainous country, on a borrowed bike. Later that same week, we pitched tents at Island Campground on the North Umpqua for five days. Walter, who'd never been in such a wild place in his life, had strong reactions. On our first evening Mike taught him to fly-cast, and he finally landed a good-sized trout that he cooked on our

Coleman stove along with trout the rest of us had caught.

What followed had to be the first campfire of his life. We talked until long after dark, when everybody but Walter climbed into sleeping bags. I fell asleep as I always do, listening to the river. Hours later, I think between 3 and 4 a.m., a noise outside woke me up. I pulled a tent flap aside and saw Walter, a smile on his face, still feeding wood to the fire.

Seeing him there brought my own first campfire to mind, on the same riverbank at Island Campground. Tired after hours of fishing, Mike and I sat on folding chairs close to the fire, taking turns adding chunks of Douglas fir when necessary. We talked about how valuable fire was in ancient cultures, a basic element of human life, along with air, water and earth. Fire still serves as an invitation to rest in comfort and security, and to think and talk. When we're physically tired after doing something we had to do or wanted to do, and we gather wood and somebody strikes a match, a fire brings pleasant relaxation and inspires clear thought. Campfires could well have been – almost had to be – the true foundation of philosophy.

***

The power of nature produced mixed results when my brother Herbert and his wife Kaethi, and Kaethi's brother Horst and his wife, visited us a few summers later and stayed in a comfortable house we'd arranged for them. When we took them out to dinner I could tell they missed their traditional German food. They didn't end up impressed with the Oregon coast – too cool, too windy - but on the way there, in Cave Junction, we drove past a saloon with bright red swinging doors just like the ones they'd seen in cowboy movies. Mike was driving, and they insisted he stop. They used all the film they had taking pictures of themselves going in and coming out through the swinging saloon doors.

After the coast trip I went with them to San Francisco and showed them around. On the drive down Interstate 5 they were all amazed at the number of pick-up trucks on the road. They wondered why so many Americans owned their own trucks and, wherever they were coming from or going to, why they were taking so much stuff with them. Somewhere between Redding and the Bay Area, Horst swerved onto the shoulder of the road and stopped. *"Da oben ist ein Haus!"* he said. (There's a house up there!) Someone not far ahead of us was towing half a doublewide trailer. Talking it over, the visitors wondered if Americans dragged entire homes up and down the road so they'd always have places to put their hauled possessions.

Back in southern Oregon, Herbert found things to enjoy. He contrasted our hikes through local forests to hikes he'd taken in the Alps, where popular trails were clogged with people. His most enjoyable experience was sighting, close-up, a large herd of elk near Howard Prairie Lake. He raved about it for days. All four of our German visitors had an unexpected experience they'll never forget when, in two cars, with Mike and I leading the way, we all drove through the Wildlife Safari in Winston, where there are 600 wild animals to view. Signs along the route warn visitors not to stop their cars, but when a black bear acted as though it wanted to cross in front of them, my brother, who couldn't read the signs, stopped. When the bear ripped their front license plate off and climbed onto the hood of their car all four occupants were understandably terrified, but, luckily, a nearby park employee quickly frightened the animal away.

Not long before they left for home I asked Kaethi what she thought of Oregon, and she answered with a single sentence: *"Wohin man auch blickt, nichts als Baume."* (Everywhere you look, there's nothing but trees.)

TWO MORE BOTTLES OF
THE MARIJUANA BEER

As late-middle-aged adults Mike and I decided to visit a new place, the small town of Manuel Antonio on the Pacific coast of Costa Rica. We'd heard good things about the country from people we knew who'd been there, and we read about it before we made the decision to go. They had a stable democracy that had disbanded its army in 1949 to invest the money saved in education and health care. (Imagine that.) Because they protect their environment instead of exploiting it, ecotourists from around the world visit their national parks and protected areas.

It was early afternoon when we landed at the San Jose airport. When I used my best Spanish to ask a lady sitting behind an airport desk for directions to a bus terminal, she told me that hiring a private driver wouldn't cost much more than bus tickets, and would be *mas rapida y mas comoda* (faster and more comfortable).

She helped me make arrangements, and she was right. For a reasonable price, a friendly young man with a clean and comfortable car drove us for three hours through lush hills where coffee beans grew, and then along a coastal plain on a road lined with coconut palms. He stopped once, on a bridge, and told me there was something we should see in the river below. When we looked over the railing there were at least a dozen crocodiles swimming and splashing around in shallow water. *"Quieres ir a nadir?"* the driver asked with a smile. (Want to go swimming?)

Our hotel was no more than ten or fifteen yards from the beach, and a short walk from the northern border of the Manuel Antonio National Park. The lush rainforest began behind a small swimming pool below our second floor room. As we unpacked and changed into swimsuits and t-shirts, bird calls sounded out of the trees. Four white faced monkeys, the first monkeys I'd ever seen outside a zoo, appeared on our balcony railing. A sign advised us not to feed monkeys, but if I'd had anything I knew they liked I'd have broken a rule and offered it to them. When we opened the door to leave for the beach, the monkeys, after looking us over, swung away through the trees, back into the forest.

I'd seen many beaches in my life by then, from the Island of Capri to the islands of Hawaii. This one was perfect – white sand, clear blue water, cumulus clouds in an otherwise clear sky, and an orange sun about to set. The month was March, the weather perfect. We swam in the warmest ocean water I'd ever experienced. While we were swimming, just before the sun disappeared behind a long line of clouds at the horizon, a group of young men and women from Canada joined us. They were in the area as volunteers to work on a coffee plantation, and had come to the beach after work. We all stayed in the water until after dark. When Mike made a cutting, funny comment about George W. Bush, one of the young women – she spoke

English with a French accent - walked through waist-deep water to shake his hand and then aggressively embrace him. Afterwards, Mike told me he thought she looked a lot like Bridget Bardot, and he wondered what more she might have done if he'd denounced Dick Cheney too.

At a nearby restaurant – five or six small tables under a thatched roof – we ate a fresh fish dinner. The waiter told us they served beer that somehow included marijuana in its brewing process, so we ordered bottles. After dinner, on the balcony outside our room, we drank two more bottles of the marijuana beer while we talked and listened to bird calls and watched geckos walking upside down and back and forth across our ceiling, using their long tongues, half again the length of their bodies, to feed on insects.

Every day for a week we hiked trails through the National Park, where we rarely encountered people, and, after we were a few miles into the rainforest, we never saw anybody. We did see deer, iguanas, three-toed sloths clinging to tree trunks, and hundreds of white faced and squirrel monkeys, many mothers carrying their young ones on their backs as they swung through the trees. Every morning, off somewhere in the distance, we heard the intimidating, low-pitched growls of howler monkeys, but we never saw one. We wanted to see Costa Rica from the sea, so spent a day on a chartered fishing boat. Out a mile or more from shore, we admired endless miles of deserted beaches stretching southward – blue water, shore-break waves, bright white sand, with dense green forest land behind it. The fact that there was no sign of civilization anywhere made it the loveliest place I've ever seen. I caught and released a sailfish, not just the biggest fish I'd ever caught in my life, but the biggest fish I'd ever seen.

Costa Rican sailfish caught and released

I can't define the calming, heartening power of raw nature to people who haven't experienced it themselves. There's no need to try to define it to people who know.

I CAN TAKE MYSELF THERE
IN MY MIND

Good and bad luck have a lot to do with most of what happens to us through our lives. Mike and I have had our share of good luck. Our son and daughter made it through their teenage years without any serious problems. Like me, Ingrid grew up an extrovert, and Pete was a somewhat shy boy – a characteristic of males on my side of the family – but, beginning in middle school, his success as a distance runner gave him assurance. Years later he would meet his wife Susan at a 10 kilometer run, and they've been married now for thirty years.

With a master's degree in environmental studies from Southern Oregon, Pete eventually became an arborist tending to 93 acres of trees in Ashland's Lithia Park. Ingrid has been an admired elementary school teacher in town for thirty years. We've camped, hiked, backpacked, fly-fished and cross-country skied together. They've blessed us with two grandsons, Billy and Jake (by way of Ingrid), and a granddaughter Dana (via Susan).

Pete and Ingrid knew my mother as Oma in Bamberg, and I became Oma in Oregon. I have countless precious memories of our grandchildren, happy experiences I know I'll be thankful for on the day I die. I liked reading books in both German and English to Dana, and

I encouraged her to join a hula group and take gymnastic lessons. Billy and Jake liked books too, but, when they were young, balloon volleyball and make-believe were their favorite indoor pastimes. Jake's favorite make-believe game was playing store, and Billy wanted to carry on long conversations with groups of stuffed animals. Mike had a basketball hoop attached to the roof over our garage door and estimates that our grandsons shot at least ten thousand baskets there.

Our rural property was ideal for playing wiffle ball with Billy and Jake. After a few years of these pseudo-baseball games, a blue spruce tree not far from the house blew down in a storm, and there were as many wiffle balls as scrub jay nests entangled in its branches. When Billy and Jake joined organized teams, from Little League through high school, we never missed a basketball or baseball game.

We took yearly family trips to eastern Oregon's Warm Springs Reservation, where we rode horses, hiked the high desert country, and swam in pools of spring water warmer than the Costa Rican sea.

As soon as they were old enough, Mike and I encouraged the grandchildren to travel on their own, and they took more journeys than we'd counted on. We got Billy started by taking him to Baja when he was nine. Looking out the plane window at the vast Sonoran Desert not long before we landed, a troubled look on his face, he asked us if we'd find anything to eat down there. About twenty-four hours later, in Loreto's Hotel El Presidente dining room, we all enjoyed a delicious dinner that featured a dorado Billy had caught that afternoon.

As a high school junior Dana was accepted as an exchange student in Germany, and I taught her the language well and know it helped her enjoy a year with a host family in the Rhine River region. While attending Regis University in Denver on a basketball scholarship, Billy spent a summer in Peru, chaperoning a choir made up of orphaned children, and then, the following year, spent his summer at the Spanish boys' camp teaching basketball to ten-year-olds. After the camp he visited Paris with his girlfriend Rebecca, whose father was stationed there as an ambassador under Barack Obama. From Paris he went to Bamberg to spend time with my family. Jake, under a program out of Portland State University, traveled to India to experience the culture, which included working at the hospice for the sick, destitute and dying established by Mother Teresa. After that, in Guatemala, he worked as a guide for a company that led backpacking tourists up and down volcanoes, and whose profits went toward helping the poor.

Grandchildren are God's way of compensating us for growing old.

Mary Waldrip

Mike and I kept going back to our favorite places. I didn't count the trips, but I know we drove the 3,000 miles from southern Oregon to Loreto and back a dozen times or more, and flew down and back almost as often. July was our favorite fishing month, with the water flat as glass at the peak of the dorado season. We saw pelicans, gulls, terns and frigate birds diving wildly for fish. We saw breaching whales, and snorkeled among multitudes of fish. We roamed the deserted beaches on Carmen, Coronado and Danzante Islands. Once, on a Carmen Island beach, we found a small, short-haired brown and white dog entangled in a tattered net, apparently abandoned there by commercial fishermen. After we freed the dog he followed us down the beach for a mile or more, tail wagging all the way to our boat. He was a charming mutt, and he rode back to Loreto with us. We talked about trying to smuggle him across the border at Tijuana but ended up deciding against it. A lot of mutts run wild in Baja, and I think that to survive they've evolved to become a smarter subspecies than pampered purebreds. The one we rescued likely found a pack to join and was better off for it in the long run.

Later that same week, walking along a Loreto beach in early morning, we watched from a distance while a boy in a group of five who looked to be ten-to-twelve-year olds tossed a small Baja mutt, a puppy, as far as he could into the sea. They all stood waiting in shallow water, and when the puppy swam back toward the beach another boy caught it and threw it again, laughing as he did it. When they all laughed, I started running, and I reached them before they could do it again.

The mind works in weird ways. Without realizing it, I screamed at them, not in English or Spanish, but in German: *"Wenn Du das noch einmal machts, werfen wir Dich in's Wasser!"* (If you do that again I'll throw you in the water!) They couldn't have understood the words, but they got the message, and they had to see Mike, a former college football player, coming up close behind me. They ran off down the beach toward town, and the puppy, once it reached shore, ran free in the opposite direction.

***

We don't drive to Baja anymore, and I miss it, but I can take myself there in my mind anytime I want. The memories I like most are experiences that made me feel fully alive. On our very first Baja trip we flew down and stayed at the Hotel El Presidente on the beach south of Loreto. We'd brought our fly rods along with the streamer flies that were supposed to attract saltwater fish, but we didn't really know much about what we hoped to do. On our first morning, our first attempt at saltwater fly fishing, we hiked south along the beach to a rugged, rocky peninsula that formed a deep, protected bay. There was a single fishing boat a half mile out – a Mexican *panga* - but no one in sight on the beach in any direction. We cast streamers from the rocks into the deep water and began hooking and releasing shiny silver mackerel with golden spots along their sides that we later learned are called sierras. The sierras must have driven schools of sardines to the surface, because birds soon arrived, gulls, pelicans and cormorants, dozens of them crashing into the water after the sardines. We stopped casting and watched. Next to arrive after the birds was a pod of six orcas, or killer whales, undoubtedly there to feed on the sierra. We stood watching, transfixed, for a long time. That was the first true illustration of life, death and raw nature I ever saw.

Ten days later, when we flew back and landed in Los Angeles, and walked down a crowded ramp and through a passageway into a mobbed terminal, it was as if we'd entered a gigantic insane asylum, or Hell itself – overheated stale air, loudspeakers blaring, hordes of people everywhere, what some people mistakenly call the real world.

**

About halfway down the Baja Peninsula is an inland oasis village far enough off the highway so that most gringos pass it by. Entering San Ignacio on a side road, you pass a surprisingly large lagoon lined with date palms. At the end of the road is a village plaza shaded by Indian laurel trees, and the stone cathedral facing the plaza dates back to 1786. The surrounding village is quiet and friendly, and as beautiful in its own unique way as any European village I've seen.

We stayed at the La Posada Hotel, which was run by descendants of Frank Fischer, a German sailor who jumped ship during World War Two and somehow ended up in San Ignacio. I remember a warm, moonlit night when Mike and I were sitting outside our $25 room and two pretty German girls wearing shorts and faded t-shirts appeared, lugging suitcases. A bus had dropped them off, and they'd walked a mile along the lonely road from the highway to reach the La Posada. Like me, they were from Bavaria, and they sat with us and we laughed and talked for hours in both German and English, and shared the Riesling wine we'd brought with us. I told the young women about the $150 I'd won in Los Angeles by betting $2 on a horse named Herr Heinz. We wondered what the odds would be on three Bavarian women meeting by chance to drink Riesling at a German hotel in the middle of the Baja peninsula.

**

One year we flew to the southern tip of the peninsula to see if we'd been missing anything Baja had to offer. In Cabo San Lucas we found lavish hotels, time-share condos for sale, and expensive restaurants, nightclubs and bars. That meant we hadn't been missing anything. What made the whole trip worthwhile was a bus ride up the Pacific coast to Todos Santos, an isolated Pacific coast Mission village founded in 1724. I'm sure travel writers have called the village charming, and it really is. A tourist attraction in that remote place, the Hotel California, inspired a popular Eagles song. Sitting on barstools at the Hotel California bar, we drank Negra Modelo beers.

After the Modelos, waiting in the shade of a tree for our return trip bus, we were lucky. Three sets of parents with a total of ten or a dozen children between them, all dressed simply in white, appeared at the bus station.

When the parents went inside, their children hung back, looking uneasy. I decided to buy them something, cookies or candy, and I approached with what I hoped would be a reassuring smile on my face. Some of them looked at me while others tried to pretend I wasn't there. I asked them in my best Spanish if they'd like some treats (*golosinas*). No one responded, so I asked if I could buy them some candy or cookies (*dulce o galletas*).

"*Ellos no hablan espanol,*" said a voice from behind me. (They don't speak Spanish.) It was a middle-aged woman, also with a smile on her face. She went on to explain that these people were *indios* (Indians) who rarely came into town, or for that matter anywhere near it.

I went into the station, where the parents were sitting in a straight line of folding chairs just inside the door, all six with their backs straight and their hands on their knees. None of them looked at me, and I had no idea what they might be doing there.

I decided to buy *galletas* because cookies, with less sugar, are at least a little more healthful than *dulces*. When I carried the cookies back outside, the children were glad to take them. They quietly glowed with innocence and gratitude.

Mike and I didn't figure the mystery out until we were back in Oregon. They must have been *Guaycura* people, Indians that have inhabited southern Baja for thousands of years, hunters and gatherers with a language unrelated to any other Native American dialect. I'll always feel privileged to have entered their lives for a few minutes.

A DAYTIME VIEW
OF MOUNTAINS

When it comes time to die, be not like those whose hearts are filled with fear of death... Sing your death song, and die like a hero going home.

MOHICAN CHIEF AUPUMUT

Mike's great-grandfather, John Brant, was descended from Mohawk Chief Joseph Brant (Thayendanegea), who fought hard, and well, against the Americans in the Revolutionary War. Two Mohawk Indians had contacted Mike about his book, *Mohawk Blood,* and wanted to visit. They arrived on a sunny summer afternoon and when the doorbell sounded both Mike and I went to the door. I was surprised, but not by the Mohawks. They were two healthy looking youngish men, and standing between them was a very large, unleashed grey-coated dog that looked to me something like an overgrown German shepherd.

Mike invited them in, and, with the animal between the Mohawks, we introduced ourselves and shook hands.

"Is the dog friendly?" I asked.

"It's not a dog," said one of the men, "it's a wolf, and she's always well behaved."

The wolf stared hard at me, and when I leaned over to scratch between her ears her black-tipped tail wagged.

We walked across the living room and out onto the deck to sit in sunlight. Mike talked to the Mohawks about a subject they politely asked him not to talk about with anybody else. I watched the wolf, sitting now between two chairs, still staring at me. A couple of minutes had passed when I saw her nose twitch. Then she stood, concentrating I could tell, something like a bird dog figuring out a scent. She walked across the deck, down three steps into the yard, and then across the yard and through the back door into our garage.

Our second golden retriever had died a few months back, and just inside the door to the garage was a plastic garbage can that still had Amber's dry dog food in it. The wolf used a front paw to pry the lid off and then lowered her head to eat. When she'd had enough she came back across the yard and deck and up the steps to sit between the same two chairs, green eyes staring at me. I stared back, wondering what, if anything, she thought about eyes of blue.

The Mohawk visitors stayed for more than an hour. Afterwards Mike and I talked about wolves, referring to books we knew. I remembered a scene from Cormac Mc-Carthy's novel *The Crossing*. Billy Parham, who'd rescued a trapped wolf and was taking it to Mexico to turn it loose in the mountains, quickly realized that wolves were smarter than dogs. What he didn't know was how much smarter. Mike showed me an Aldo Leopold quote. As a young man Leopold had shot a wolf from a long distance, and then came this: *"We reached the old wolf in time to watch a fierce green light dying in her eyes. I realized then and have known ever since that there was something new to me in those eyes, something known only to her and the mountain."*

The wolf that came to visit taught me what Leopold meant.

———————

"Deserve's got nothing to do with it."

CLINT EASTWOOD,
IN *UNFORGIVEN*

———————

It was springtime, and in August I'd turn eighty years old, an age that not so long ago had sounded almost prehistoric to me. Even though I did almost everything people are encouraged to do to stay healthy, I worried about my age.

In bed late on a Saturday night I woke up short of breath with pain across my shoulders. I woke Mike up and told him what was wrong, and that I thought we should go to the emergency room. I saw that he was shocked.

In a matter of minutes we were dressed and on the road, driving the dark, deserted highway 66 toward town. When we reached town the lighted streets were empty, and all the way to the hospital Mike tried to reassure me. At the north edge of town we climbed the hill to the hospital, where an ambulance was stationed outside the emergency room door and three or four cars were parked in the lot.

Just inside the door a middle-aged nurse sat behind a desk reading a book, and I heard a woman's voice coming from somewhere behind her, but I couldn't understand what was being said. I told the nurse about my shoulder pain and shortness of breath and that I thought it could be a heart attack. Looking cool and concerned at the same time, she turned her book over to keep her place.

"Who's your family doctor?" she asked.

I told her.

"Please, come with me," she said, and I did, with Mike behind us.

She led us into a typical small hospital room with a desk, an examination table and two chairs.

"Sit down, please," she said on her way out. "The doctor will be here in just a minute."

We sat in the chairs, and now I could clearly hear the woman's voice I'd heard before. She must have been talking to a nurse in the next room, and their door was open.

"I need to go home," the expressionless voice said. "Can I go home?"

"Do you know anyone in town?" the nurse asked. "Anyone who could pick you up and give you a ride home?"

"I don't think I do."

"Do you live in town?"

"Maybe. Maybe not. I think so. I used to. Is anything wrong with me?"

"How did you get here?" asked the nurse.

"I don't remember. Can anybody help me?"

"Can you think of anyone you know? A family member? A friend?"

"I don't know if I have any friends left. I used to have a son."

The doctor, a short, heavyset man in an unbuttoned white coat with a stethoscope around his neck, hurried through our door and closed it. He introduced himself, but I didn't get his name.

He told Mike to please wait outside. Then, as he used the stethoscope, he asked me if I'd experienced jaw pains, sweating, dizziness, fatigue, or indigestion.

I told him no.

"Your heart sounds fine. Exceptional in fact. Please, come with me. We'll see what we can find out."

Outside the small room he told Mike to please wait in what he called the lobby. "We won't be long," he said.

He led me down a long, quiet hallway. I was frightened and nervous. Near the end of the hallway he showed me into a slightly larger room.

"We need some images," the doctor said. "But your heart seems to be fine."

Standing in front of what I assumed was an x-ray machine, I turned at different angles, and after each turn the machine beeped as the doctor got his images. If my heart was healthy, what could be wrong? Cancer came to mind. Because of something I'd read – I couldn't remember where - I found myself wondering if the radiation treatments I'd undergone for breast cancer might have caused cancer in my right lung. No, I told myself. Then I remembered that Mike, Ingrid and I had visited Germany not long after the Chernobyl nuclear disaster in 1986. I'd read somewhere that cancer rates had increased across Europe after that. No, I told myself again. Not that. I don't deserve cancer again.

Fifteen minutes later we were back on the lonely, lighted streets through town.

"He thinks you're all right," Mike said. "You know how glad I am. I wonder what could've caused the pain. The symptoms."

"Old age?"

"Maybe. But I'm almost a year older than you."

We both tried to laugh.

During breakfast on Monday morning our landline phone rang. We get our share of typical scam calls – everything from imaginary Amazon bills to a kidnapped grandchild – so we ordinarily ignore the phone unless we have a reason to expect a call. I hurried to the kitchen, and answered when I saw our doctor's name on the screen. His nurse was on the line and told me that the doctor would like to see me at nine o'clock, if possible, and to bring Mike along.

The doctor told me he was sorry, and I knew he meant it, when he showed us the dark image he thought was cancer of my right lung on his computer screen. When he told me where I'd have to go next and what to expect, I was too anxious to pay attention. Before we left the nurse gave us printed instructions, and I read them over twice on the way home.

A few days later, after a biopsy, what could be called good news came by phone. I had non-small cell lung cancer, and surgery could treat it. Leading up to the surgery, I was sometimes frightened, sometimes confused, and often angry. I'd never smoked, I'd run marathons, I was physically fit, I breathed more fresh air than most people on earth did. And now I thought I might soon die. No, I didn't deserve it.

The oncologist assigned to me, a young doctor from India, was confident and friendly. He explained that, after surgery, I'd most likely qualify for immunotherapy, so wouldn't have to deal with chemotherapy and its well known consequences – fatigue, nausea, hair loss, mouth sores, hearing and heart problems.

On a sunny morning, Mike drove me fifteen miles down the road to the hospital in Medford, with Ingrid in the back seat. Instead of talking about where we were going and what would happen there, we made small talk about unimportant matters – trips we'd taken, books we'd read, movies we'd seen, songs we liked.

After I was signed in and led away, I felt entirely alone. My memories of what happened are hazy, as if I'd been in a trance. I know I ended up in a large room with beds lining the walls. Men and women, young and old – mostly old - were waiting for their surgeries. A nurse handed me a plastic bag and showed me into a cubicle where I undressed and, with her help, put on a hospital gown.

Back out of the cubicle, lying on a bed, I remember getting injections that, almost immediately, made me feel as if I'd had too much wine. Soon I was wheeled down a long corridor and into what I knew had to be an operating room.

They put me to sleep, and then I woke up looking at a white ceiling.

"Am I supposed to be awake?" I said to no one.

Then a nurse was there. "Yes you are," she said. "You're all done now, honey. Relax."

She rearranged my pillow and I fell asleep.

It might have been ten minutes or two hours when I woke up again. Mike and Ingrid were standing close beside the bed, smiling down at me.

"The doctor told me everything went well," Mike said. "In fact he said perfectly. How do you feel?"

"You'll be okay!" Ingrid said. "I love you, mom!"

As best I could, I smiled back.

I spent four nights in the hospital, feeling lucky to have a daytime view of mountains through the only window in my room. I didn't experience great pain, but I felt weak. During the first day and night nurses fed me, brought me water, gave me pills, checked my blood pressure, helped me in and out of the bathroom. Every so often they got me out of bed and, for five or ten minutes at a time, walked me up and down a hallway.

The door to my room stayed open day and night, and there was a nurses' station not far from the door. During my first night, I had no choice but to listen to three nurses talking.

"How come we get the lousy shifts so often?"

"Seniority."

"Lack of it you mean."

"More like favoritism?"

"We ought to get paid double for overtime."

"I think we make good enough money."

"No we don't."

"I'd call it good money."

"Are you kidding? The doctors make the real money around here."

Mike, Pete and Ingrid visited as often as visiting hours allowed. My surgeon came by on my fourth morning, checked my bandages, and told me everything was looking very good. There were no complications or unexpected aftereffects.

"Should we keep you here over the weekend?" he asked.

"No," I said.

"All right then. You're fit to go."

Not long after the doctor left a nurse gave me more printed instructions and wished me well. I recognized her voice as the one who'd complained that doctors make the real money.

By mid-morning, when I was dressed and ready to go home, a male nurse came into my room pushing a wheelchair.

"I can walk," I told him.

"I believe you," he said. "But we have these rules."

With Mike and Ingrid at my sides, he wheeled me down a long hallway, into an elevator, then along another hallway to the outside door.

The car was parked nearby. Out of the antiseptic hospital smell, the simple act of walking on my own through fresh air felt wonderful.

A BABY HAD JUST
BEEN BORN

*Sometimes you got to listen hard for the sounds old
Mother Earth makes, all on her own.*

GREG BROWN, FROM THE SONG *EUGENE*

M y quick recovery surprised my doctors. In the beginning I reported to the hospital every three weeks
for immunotherapy, which meant half-hour long infusions of a new cancer drug called keytruda. Until the
covid pandemic arrived Mike always sat with me in the
infusion rooms - large rooms with lots of windows, the
walls lined with padded chairs always occupied with patients. I didn't find the depressing environment I'd antic-
ipated there. Brave patients were inspirational. There was
a calm, beautiful, pregnant young woman with a friendly
look on her face who, during my first infusion, was treated with chemotherapy in the chair next to mine. During
our conversation she explained that radiation was more
dangerous than chemo for her baby. There were patients

who succeeded in cheering one another up, and old men and women who cracked jokes. The nurses were always kind and helpful. Nearly all infusion room patients smiled along with the nurses when Brahms Lullaby was played over the hospital sound system, meaning that a baby had just been born.

After four months of tri-weekly infusions my scans looked good enough for my oncologist to recommend six week intervals between treatments, a schedule I'll likely be on for the rest of my life. The only annoying keytruda side effect I experience is arthritis pain.

***

Nearly all of Mike's old friends have died, and many of mine have too. Others have moved away, and all three of our grandchildren have left Oregon to make their adult lives in other places. Pete and Ingrid are still in Ashland, and my book club still meets on the second Tuesday of the month. I join my financial aid office friends for wine and conversation three or four times in a year, and I'm thankful that Inge, always my closest German friend, is still in town.

I don't run marathons, or cross-country ski, or hike rough country looking for mountain quail. I don't wade the North Umpqua casting for summer steelhead. Even if I did, accelerated climate change has drastically reduced the steelhead runs. The 2021 Jack Creek wildfire obliterated the Moores' log house along with the five rental houses on their property, including our cabin. Frank died at age ninety-nine in 2022, and Jeanne lives with her daughter downriver in the small town of Glide. Neither Mike nor I are sorry that we'll likely never board another airplane as long as we live. We did our traveling when it made the most sense to us, when we were young enough (and also old enough) to truly enjoy it.

My last trip back to Germany was supposed to happen in July, 2016, but what happened instead strengthened my distaste for air travel. That was the summer that grandson Billy was in Spain. My plan was to stay with my sister in Nurnberg, and Billy's plan was to come from Spain and meet us there. From Nurnberg we'd drive north to Bamberg, and I'd show him where I grew up and all the special places Mike and I loved. But at the Medford airport the clerk behind the United Airlines counter told me matter-of-factly that I couldn't travel out of the country. The expiration date on my passport wasn't quite six months away. The fact that the expiration date would be five full months beyond the return date on my roundtrip ticket didn't matter. I was the innocent victim of a bureaucratic rule that couldn't possibly have made sense to anybody, and it spoiled our plans. So Billy, who didn't speak a word of German, visited my sister, who didn't speak a word of English. As always, she was kind and generous, and they got along well despite the circumstances. With a newly issued passport, I visited my sister in September. I missed Mike and again realized, more clearly than ever, that Oregon was where I belonged.

In December, 2019, at age eighty-two, Mike took his last long road trip, the 1,500 miles from Ashland to Loreto with our youngest grandson, Jake, twenty-one years old at the time. They camped, fished and explored Baja together, and came back to Oregon just in time for Christmas, a few short weeks before covid arrived.

We still enjoy short road trips, often with part or all of our extended family. Our favorite destination is the coast. The inexpensive motel we like is isolated, with miles of beach to roam in either direction. The other guests there are almost always people we have things in common with. Last summer Ingrid drove us over with Billy and Jake. Before we reached the ocean we stopped for an hour to walk among the redwoods.

I know what every colored woman in this world is doing – Dying. Just like me. But the difference is they dying like a stump. I'm going down like one of those redwoods. I sure did live in this world.

Toni Morrison

We checked into our rooms in early afternoon and then, in warm weather under a clear sky, we hiked south, toward distant hills. It was an ebb tide, so the wet sand was hard-packed for easy walking. Sand dollars lay everywhere, and gulls, keeping just ahead of us, were feeding on dead crabs that lay on the wet sand. When we finally reached the hills we encountered a herd of elk feeding on ferns.

After the hike we drove north on the coast highway to a Mexican restaurant we knew. It was dark by the time we got back to the motel, and we saw that, as usual, nearly all the guests were outside, facing the ocean in comfortable chairs provided on the long wooden deck that served every room. They were talking and laughing, some drinking wine or beer. With the ocean no more than thirty yards away, breaking waves showed phosphorescence in the darkness.

Pulling into the motel lot, we'd parked next to a shiny black Harley Davidson motorcycle. Sometimes stereotypes come true. The cyclist's room was three doors from ours. He could have passed for an old-school Hell's Angel - a big, long-haired, scraggly bearded, tattooed middle-aged man dressed in black. But that was where the stereotype ended. He was friendly and well-spoken, and did his best to make friends with everybody. Somewhere along the road he'd bought a giant watermelon, and used his hunting knife to carve it up and deliver a piece to everybody who wanted one, up and down the line. Not long after the watermelon had been distributed a full moon rose over the mountains behind us, making it light enough to clearly see the eternally breaking waves.

***

Every morning at home, Mike distributes seeds for the birds out on our deck before breakfast, and we watch them through the glass door. By the time I'm done eating I usually have our old cat Dingbat curled up on my old lap. He's been trained not to bother birds, but he likes to watch them too.

Later, after the breakfast dishes are washed, we walk a few miles in one or another of our preferred locations. On one of my favorite routes, about a mile from home we cross an earthen dam at Emigrant Lake, climb a hill, pass by a pioneer cemetery with gravestones that date to the 1800s, and then finally circle back to re-cross the dam. Depending on the season of the year, we might see flocks of geese and mallard ducks, or bald eagles, or high-flying hawks and turkey vultures.

Back home, out on the deck when the weather is nice - or inside when it's not - we drink coffee or tea and talk, but not for very long, about the consistently gloomy news in the morning paper. We meditate before lunch - it helps us handle the morning news - and after lunch we read or write, and play chess, and nearly every day I find an hour to play my zither.

I regularly talk by phone with my sister and my old friend Ingrid in Germany. Friends and family visit us on Reiten Drive often, including friends a generation younger, who keep us feeling younger too. In 2020 our extended family shared Covid Christmas dinner in our garage, with the door open to a sunny day, and portable heaters that kept the temperature pleasant. I sat close to the open garage door so I could see the Siskiyou Mountains. The following May, Mike and I had a back yard party to celebrate our 60th wedding anniversary, with familiar mountain views in three directions. Mercifully, as the state of the world deteriorates, mountains somehow make me stronger. I believe the mountains have become a part of me. Does my imagination do that? Could it be a version of the placebo effect? Does that really matter? No.

When despair for the world grieves in me and I wake in the night at the least sound in fear of what my children's lives may be, I go and lie down where the wood drake rests in his beauty on the water, and the great heron feeds. I come into the peace of wild things who do not tax their lives with forethought of grief.

WENDELL BERRY